OREGON
ROAD TRIPS

OREGON COAST
EDITION

Discover Oregon! Mike & Kristy

MIKE & KRISTY WESTBY

Discover the Oregon Coast by Day –
Stay in Historic Hotels by Night™

The majority of photos within
this book are copyright Mike & Kristy Westby

ISBN-13: 978-0998395036

102620b - CS

Cover graphics by Sarah Craig – SarahCookDesign.com

"And above all, watch with glittering eyes the whole world around you, because the greatest secrets are always hidden in the most unlikely places."

Roald Dahl

Follow
Discover-Oregon

Yaquina Head Lighthouse

On the Web:
www.Discover-Oregon.com

On Twitter:
@DiscoverOre.com

On Facebook:
www.Facebook.com/DiscoverORE

On Instagram:
DiscoverOregon4300

OREGON ROAD TRIPS - OREGON COAST EDITION

Discover the Oregon Coast!

An exciting 9-day vacation exploring the Oregon Coast is now as easy as 1-2-3...

1) Write in the Dates of Your Trip
2) Make Your Hotel Reservations
3) Pack Your Bags and Go!

Using this easy-to-use guide, you'll simply turn each page as you motor along and choose which points of interest to stop at and explore during your day's journey, *all while making your way towards that evening's stay at a historic Oregon hotel.*

An exciting vacation awaits...and it's already planned for you!

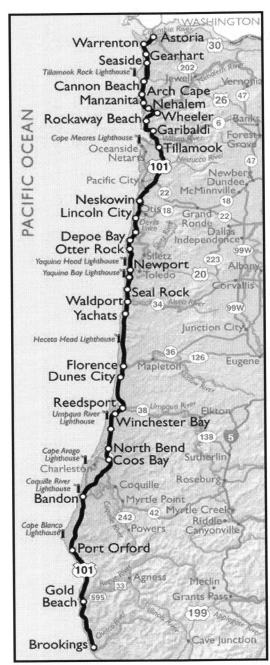

Map Courtesy of www.TravelOregon.com

YOUR JOURNEY

INTRODUCTION

Shore Acres State Park

Oregon is a vast and beautiful state. I could list its square mileage, its demographics or perhaps the distance from border to border, but a better description is...it starts with the shores of the Pacific Ocean on its western edge, traverses east over the Oregon Coast Range and into the verdant Willamette Valley, climbs over the snowy summits of the Cascade mountain range while skirting south of the sublime Columbia River Gorge and then continues forever into the remote, silent and dramatic beauty and history of eastern Oregon.

This guide is about setting out on your own adventure to explore the Oregon coast. It's about the journey, not the destination. It's about asking, "I wonder where that goes?" It's about hitting the brakes and turning off the pavement. Opening a door and saying "Hello". Shutting off the engine, getting out of the car and gazing over the never-ending expanse that is the Pacific Ocean. It's about climbing the stairs of a lighthouse, marveling at the spout of a gray whale, cracking open a buttery claw of a Dungeness Crab, and losing sense of time while walking for miles along a sandy beach as the waves applaud your sense of adventure.

HOW TO BEGIN

At over 360 miles in length, the Oregon Coast's immense size, historical treasures and abundance of geographical features are too much to capture in one trip. In fact, its countless riches can be so intimidating that travelers don't know where to begin...so they don't. Analysis paralysis.

Good news! This book already has your route planned for you. There are only three simple things you need to do...

1) Select the 9-day period for your trip and write those dates into this book at the beginning of each chapter.

2) Call and make reservations at the historic hotels found at the end of each day, which correspond with your chosen dates.

3) Pack your bags, hop in the car and simply choose the sights you wish to stop at and explore each day as you motor along.

Note that some of the optional activities you'll enjoy during your trip, such as riding in the cab of a 1925 steam locomotive or whale watching from a charter boat, will also require reservations, and these are noted at the beginning of each chapter/day.

www.Discover-Oregon.com

TIMING

Your Oregon Coast road trip is a beautiful journey anytime of the year, with the conditions changing dramatically from season to season. Spring, summer and fall bring some of the finest weather in Oregon, as well as the entire United States, while winter can produce brooding or stormy skies, perfect for exploring shops, enjoying a bowl of warm clam chowder by a window in a small restaurant, or simply reading a book in your hotel room while under a blanket beside a warm fire.

WHERE TO START

The "official" first stop of your 9-day road trip is in Astoria, Oregon, at the northern edge of the Oregon coast. If it works with your schedule, we recommend you travel to Astoria the day before you begin and stay the night at the historic Cannery Pier Hotel & Spa. See Page 21 for additional details.

NORTH TO SOUTH

Your journey along the Oregon Coast can obviously be done driving north to south or south to north. We opted to create this guide taking travelers north to south so as to make most of the turns off and back onto Hwy 101 an easy right turn.

THEY'RE YOUR BEACHES

In 1967, Oregon passed what is known as *The Beach Bill*, which declared that all of Oregon's beaches belong to the public. As a result, none of Oregon's beaches are privately owned, and all visitors to the Oregon Coast may enjoy any and all of Oregon's beautiful beaches without restriction.

Add or Remove a Day to Customize Your Trip

This 9-day road trip of the Oregon Coast can actually be any length you'd like. Want to shorten it to 7 days, or perhaps 5? Then begin your trip on Day 4 instead of Day 1, or simply combine a couple of days into one and visit only those destinations you'll have time for. Want to stretch it out for more than 9 days? Then stay an extra day in your hotel at Newport, Bandon or Cannon Beach, or add a night in a quaint coastal town, such as Oceanside or Yachats.

Whale Watching

You can expect to see some whales during your trip, as nearly 20,000 gray whales migrate up and down the coast year-round, with most being spotted from mid-December through January, from late March to June, and then through the summer months, with September being a high point of the year. Fortunately, most of the destinations you visit in this book, such as Cape Lookout, Cape Perpetua, and Yaquina Head, are perfect for spotting whales. See the article titled *Whale Watching on the Oregon Coast* on Page 190 to learn more about this exciting and memorable Oregon tradition.

Make Your Reservations

Sunset from Depoe Bay

These are the reservations you will need to make for your trip. All necessary lodging reservations are shown in bold. All others are optional activities.

Night 1 – Stay at The Cannery Pier Hotel & Spa

- **Cannery Pier Hotel & Spa - 503-325-4996**

Day 1 – Astoria, OR to Cannon Beach, OR

Make a reservation for 1 night

- **The Cannon Beach Hotel – 503-436-1392**
- or The Stephanie Inn – 503-436-2221
- or The Ocean Lodge – 503-436-2241

Day 2 – Cannon Beach, OR to Tillamook, OR

Make a reservation for 1 night

- **Sheltered Nook Tiny Homes – 503-805-5526**
- Oregon Coast Railriders – Reserve online at www.OCRailriders.com or 541-786-6165

Day 3 – Tillamook, OR to Depoe Bay, OR

Make a reservation for 1 night

- **The Channel House – 541-765-2140**
- or The Whale Cove Inn – 541-765-4300
- Oregon Coast Scenic Railroad – Reservation to ride in the locomotive cab - 503-842-7972

Day 4 – Depoe Bay, OR to Newport, OR

Make a reservation for 1 night

- **Sylvia Beach Hotel B & B: 541-765-4300**
- Ocean House Bed & Breakfast – 541-265-3888
- Carrie's Whale Watching EcoExcursions – 541-912-6734 or book online at www.OregonWhales.com
- Marine Discovery Cruise – Newport – 541-265-6200

Day 5 – Newport, OR to Heceta Head

Make a reservation for 1 night

- **Heceta Head Lighthouse B & B – 541-547-3696 – 1-866-547-3696 or www.HecetaLighthouse.com**

Day 6 – Heceta Head to Coos Bay, OR

Make a reservation for 1 night

- **The Coos Bay Manor – 541-269-1224**

Day 7 – Coos Bay, OR to Bandon, OR

Make a reservation for 1 night

- **Bandon Dunes Golf Resort – 1-800-742-0172**

Day 8 – Bandon, OR to Gold Beach, OR

You'll be making reservations for **1 or 2 nights** this evening.

- **1 Night** – In this case, you'll stay tonight in Gold Beach, enjoy the Rogue River Jet Boats tomorrow during Day 9, and then start your drive home immediately afterwards.

- **2 Nights** – In this case, you'll stay in Gold Beach tonight and, instead of driving home tomorrow after enjoying your Rogue River jet boat tour, you'll stay a second night at a hotel of your choice, be it in Gold Beach or elsewhere. See more about this option on Page 186 before making your reservations for this evening's stay.

- **Rogue River Lodge at Snag Patch – 541-247-0101**
- or Tu Tu' Tun Lodge – 541-247-6664
- or Pacific Reef Resort – 541-247-6658

Day 9 – Gold Beach, OR

Drive home today after experiencing the thrills of Jerry's Rogue River Jets or stay at the hotel you selected in the choices above, under Day 8.

- **Drive home or stay at** _____
- Jerry's Rogue River Jetboat Tours – 800-451-3645

SOME GROUND RULES

"It's the Journey, Not the Destination."

The key to your journey is to alter your driving mindset. It really isn't about getting *there*, it's about discovering *here*. With this in mind, here are some ground rules to follow...

- Get used to stopping the car and getting out.
- Now stop the car and get out.
- Stop the car and get out...again. You'll be glad you did.
- Always ask "I wonder where that goes?"...and go there.
- Hit the brakes and turn right.
- Open the door and say "Hello."
- Don't assume it has to be a short conversation.
- Never mind that you just stopped back there...stop again here.
- Yes, it is a nice view. Feel free to stop, get out and admire it.
- This very moment is the time to do it. You won't be coming back this way next week.
- Enjoy the journey!

Travel Beyond the Page

By all means, do not feel you have to stop at only the places found in this book, as there are many more than those listed here just waiting to be discovered. Go ahead...follow that narrow lane, stop at that small museum, walk the trail to the viewpoint, and open the door to the shop that looks closed, but isn't. It's all about taking the time to...discover Oregon.

The Same, But Different

Following the information in this guide, you will enjoy a unique and exciting vacation discovering the Oregon Coast. It's important to note, however, that with a little creativity, you can also make this same journey a second or third time and have it be an almost entirely new and different trip each time. With trip number one, you may find you have only enough time in your day to explore the Astoria Column, the Yaquina Head Lighthouse and Cape Perpetua, leaving the Tillamook County Museum, Oregon Coast Scenic Railroad and the Oregon Coast Aquarium completely undiscovered. That means they'll all be waiting when you make your next trip!

Feel Free to Add a Day or Two

Keep in mind as you book your reservations that you can extend your road trip simply by booking a hotel reservation for two nights instead of one. This way, you'll have more time to explore the local area, rent a boat to go crabbing, stroll through some shops, hike a nearby trail, and enjoy a leisurely dinner.

"So, Where Are You From?"

There are many blessings on a trip like this, one of which is the number of conversations you simply fall into. It usually begins with a simple question or comment, and the next thing you know, you're involved in a 30-minute conversation with some of the nicest people you've ever met. Why? Because the folks you meet on a trip like this are your neighbors, it's just that they're a quite a few houses further down the block. If you approach a town, café, museum or someone with an air of traveling arrogance, then you're making a huge mistake. Instead, be genuine and friendly. You'll be amazed at how many people you'll meet and how pleasant your trip will be.

And in those rare instances where you meet someone who loves to talk...about themselves...then excuse yourselves with the tried and true "Well, we need to be hitting the road if we're going to stay on schedule."

Get Some Good *Paper* Maps

We can't emphasize this enough. You will want to travel with and use a couple of good paper maps, and the more detailed, the better. Your phone will no doubt work well, but you're setting out to explore some remote parts of the Oregon Coast, many of which have no cell signal whatsoever, so your phone will not work there. In addition, your paper maps will always boot up and never run out of power.

As you make your way along and stop at various locations, you'll often see folded Oregon maps made available for free by the Oregon Department of Transportation. These are very helpful, so grab more than one and keep them with you at all times. For more detail on the roads you'll be traveling, we also recommend the large Oregon atlases put out by DeLorme. You can find them online for about $25.

Oregon's tourism division, Travel Oregon, also issues very helpful maps, magazines and trip guides. We highly recommend you visit their web site, www.TravelOregon.com, to order some of these free guides before setting out on your trip. Especially helpful is their large *Oregon Scenic Byways Official Driving Guide.*

If you are a member of AAA, check their resources, as well. By the way, make sure your membership is up-to-date.

Coastal Parking Permits

Some of the more popular Oregon State Parks, Recreation Areas, Trail Heads, Scenic Areas, etc. charge a parking fee, and this varies from $5 for a daily permit, to $35 for an annual permit, depending upon the type of permit purchased. Note that some non-annual permits are valid for five to seven days, so they may be used at multiple sites along your road trip.

Oregon State Parks Day-Use Parking Permit – Daily: $5 – Annual: $30 – This permit is honored at all 26 Oregon State Parks that charge a parking fee. Permits are available at self-service kiosks, park booths, or offices located at the site in which a permit is required. In addition, they may be purchased by calling 800-551-6949. If you're camping, you do not need a parking permit. Just display your current state park camping receipt on your dashboard.

Oregon Pacific Coast Passport – 5-Day Permit: $10.00 – Annual Permit: $35.00. A day use permit that covers vehicle parking and day use fees for over 15 sites along Hwy 101, (the Pacific Coast Scenic Byway) including Shore Acres, Cape Lookout, Yaquina Head Outstanding Natural Area, Heceta Head and more. Available for purchase at sites along the coast, as well as by calling 800-551-6949.

Bring Your Binoculars

From sweeping panoramic vistas and off shore sea stacks to lazing seals and passing whales, there is much to see during your Oregon Coast road trip, and a good pair of binoculars will bring much of it closer to you, so be sure to bring a pair for use throughout your trip.

The Time of Year Makes a Difference

Your Discover Oregon journey is a trip best made during mid-spring to late fall, when temperatures are warm, the skies are blue, and the days are longer.   Winter can bring days of brilliant sunshine, but also many days in a row of gray weather, wind and rain. In addition, rain can fall in abundance in the springtime, so check your weather forecast.

Note that many tourist related attractions open for the summer season beginning with Memorial Day Weekend at the end of May. Make this trip even one week earlier and you may find quite a few attractions are closed until then. That said, the Oregon Coast is perfect for exploring during the "shoulder months" when there are fewer crowds and less traffic.

Six Hours Per Day – Your Results May Vary

As we've said, it's all about the journey and not the destination. That said, we found that after about six hours of being on the road, we were flipping this mantra and were ready to reach our destination. Our willingness to stop and explore was being replaced by a desire to simply reach our hotel, relax and "be there."   Everybody's results will certainly vary, especially after a nice long walk on the beach, but we found that about six hours on the road was enough for a day.

Take Your Time and Enjoy the Sights

 As you make your way through this book, you'll see a small clock icon placed next to some of the listings. There are many Oregon Coast attractions that do not require much time to visit. A stop at The Olde Telephone Company in Newport may require about half an hour, while a stop at Simpson Beach to see the hundreds of seals on the rocks may require half that, but locations and attractions such as Cape Perpetua, Oswald West State Park, Yaquina Head Lighthouse and the Oregon Coast Scenic Railway absolutely call for you to spend more time enjoying the commanding views or once-in-a-lifetime experiences. Wherever you see the clock icon, plan on spending at least an hour at that location, and we would encourage you to spend even more time there while enjoying the view, walking the beach or even riding the rails in the cab of an old steam engine. If it means missing out on some of the other stops, then so be it. They'll be waiting for you on your next Oregon Coast road trip!

We'd Love to Hear About Your Trip!

It's one thing to spend time on the road followed by months in front of a computer screen doing research, writing and turning all of this information into a book, but it's an entirely different experience to hear from real people "out in the field" discovering Oregon. What kind of fun are you having? Where did you go? What did you like best? What did you not like at all? What do you think we should add to the book? Do not hesitate to send us a note *or a photo* of your adventures at ContactUs@Discover-Oregon.com. We'd love to hear from you!

AN EARLY
START IN ASTORIA?

The first morning of your 9-day road trip along the Oregon coast begins at its northern edge, in Astoria, a town rich with history tied to the ocean and the mighty Columbia River. Filled with many things to see and do, it will take much of a day to experience.

To add a fun start to your road trip, you may want to consider staying at the Cannery Pier Hotel & Spa the night before you begin. By doing so, you can wake up the next morning, enjoy breakfast at the hotel or a nearby restaurant, and then begin the first day of your trip.

Though completely rebuilt from the piers up, the Cannery Pier Hotel has a history that reaches back over 120 years to 1897.

Guests will find well-appointed luxurious rooms featuring a cozy fireplace and a private balcony with close up views of large ocean-going ships passing beneath the massive Astoria-Megler Bridge as they make their way out to sea.

During our stay at the hotel, we enjoyed being chauffeured to and from our evening's dinner in the hotel's beautiful 1952 Cadillac DeVille. It's the perfect way to arrive in style, and it's available to all hotel guests simply by asking.

> The Cannery Pier Hotel & Spa
> No. 10 Basin Street
> Astoria, OR 97103
> 503-325-4996

Note: There is much to see and do in the Astoria area, so if you decide to begin your trip with an evening at The Cannery Pier Hotel & Spa, you may wish to arrive early enough in the day to explore the area.

Lodging Option: Hotel Elliott Astoria

Offering 32 beautifully restored rooms and suites, the historic Hotel Elliott Astoria blends 20th century elegance with today's modern amenities, all with an upscale yet relaxed feel. Each room welcomes guests with deluxe accommodations, including rich linens, heated bathroom floor tiles, handcrafted cabinetry and their signature "Wonderful Beds", all embraced within rich and warm colors. Fireplaces and two-person soaking tubs are also available in select rooms and suites.

> Hotel Elliott Astoria
> 357 12th Street
> Astoria, OR 97103
> 503-325-2222

Additional Astoria Lodging Options

In addition to the Cannery Pier Hotel and the Hotel Elliott
Astoria, you may also wish to consider these historic hotels.

Benjamin Young Inn
3652 Duane Street
Astoria, OR 97103
503-325-6172

Commodore Hotel Astoria
258 14th Street
Astoria, OR 97103
503-325-4747

Clementine's Bed & Breakfast
847 Exchange Street
Astoria, OR 97103
503-325-2005

www.Discover-Oregon.com

Day One

Astoria to
Cannon Beach

Tillamook Lighthouse

DAY 1
ASTORIA TO
CANNON BEACH

Day 1 – Date: /   /

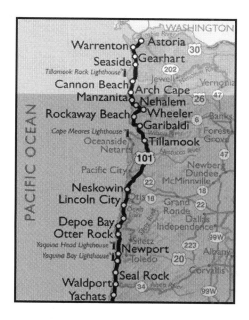

Summary: Where You're Going Today:

- Astoria, OR
- Seaside, OR
- Ecola State Park
- Cannon Beach, OR

Your 9-Day Oregon Coast road trip begins
with Astoria. Located at the northwest tip of Oregon, where
the mighty Columbia River drains into the Pacific Ocean,
Astoria has a history built upon sea-going commerce. In
addition to being a key port for the shipping of wood, grains,
and other exports around the world, as well as imported goods

to the northwest interior, the town was known as the salmon canning capital of the world, supporting 30 different companies canning Chinook, Sockeye and Coho salmon in abundant quantities from the mid-1800s to the mid-1900s.

Tonight's Lodging:

- The 1914 Cannon Beach Hotel

Today's Mileage:

- 26 Miles from Astoria to Cannon Beach

Reservations Needed for This Segment:

- The 1914 Cannon Beach Hotel – 503-436-1392 – 1 Night

Before You Leave:

Fill your gas tank in Astoria.

Start

After discovering Astoria this morning, you'll begin making your way south on Hwy 101, also known as the scenic Oregon Coast Highway. Your primary route of travel for the next 9 days, you'll follow this southwest out of town before getting your first glimpses of the beautiful Oregon coast. After a day of exploring the coast, visiting Seaside, OR, hiking at Ecola State Park, and more, you'll arrive at your destination for the evening, the historic 1914 Cannon Beach Hotel.

Note: Day 1 is a busy day, so you'll want to get an early start. There is a lot to fit into one day, and chances are you will have to save some attractions and destinations for your next visit.

☐ First Stop: Astoria Riverwalk

 Covering 6.4 miles along the Columbia River is the Astoria Riverwalk. Formerly an old rail line, today it has been converted into a level paved pathway that allows visitors to stroll or bike their way beneath the towering Astoria- Megler bridge and past restaurants, antique shops, gift shops, cannery museums, breweries, river viewpoints, docks with barking sea lions, and more. It's a perfect way to reach the Columbia River Maritime Museum and experience the active river front area of Astoria. And if you are walking instead of riding a bike, and you feel like taking a break, then hop aboard "Old 300", a colorful 1913 trolley which plys the tracks from noon to 6:00 p.m. along the Riverwalk every day, depending upon the weather. For only $1, you can hop aboard, sit down, relax and take in the sights. For only $2, you can hop on and off all day as much as you'd like. Note that you can ride the trolley round-trip, which takes about one hour.

Tip: If you're staying at the Cannery Pier Hotel, then inquire about borrowing their bikes for a casual yet speedy way to enjoy the Riverwalk.

Directions: The Astoria Riverwalk runs right along the river. Leave the hotel and find it crossing near the entrance to the hotel's pier. We recommend you travel east. If you aren't riding bikes from the hotel and want to use the trolley, you may board the trolley at any of the trolley stops along the riverfront between Basin Street, near the Astoria Riverwalk Inn, and 39th street, or simply flag down the trolley along the route.

www.Discover-Oregon.com

☐ **Next Stop:** Columbia River Maritime Museum

Located on the Astoria Riverwalk next to the Columbia River is the modern Columbia River Maritime Museum, recognized as one of the finest museums in the state. Filled with dramatic displays and interactive exhibits, the museum allows visitors to learn all about the legendary Columbia River Bar. Here, the powerful force of the mighty Columbia River meets the strength of the even mightier Pacific Ocean to create one of the most dangerous passages in the world, one in which vessels large and small must at times navigate waves reaching

40' in height during fierce winter storms. Docked nearby is the Columbia Lightship, which was stationed as a floating lighthouse 5.2 statute miles from the mouth of the Columbia River from 1951 to 1979. Visitors are welcome to board and tour the vessel as part of the museum experience.

Columbia River Maritime Museum
1792 Marine Drive
Astoria, OR 97103
503-325-2323

- Open Monday through Friday – 9:30 a.m. to 5:00 p.m.
- Admission: Adults: $14.00 – Seniors: $12.00 – Children 6 and over: $5.00.

Directions: You'll find the Columbia River Maritime Museum on the Riverwalk about 1.5 miles east of the Cannery Pier Hotel.

☐ Next Stop: The Astoria Column

Towering 125' atop 600' high Coxcomb Hill in Astoria is the colorful Astoria Column. Built in 1926 and one of Oregon's most visited parks, the column rewards those who climb its 164 steps with a commanding view of Astoria, Young's Bay, the Astoria-Megler Bridge, the Coast Range, the Columbia River and the Pacific Ocean. And just for fun, aspiring pilots, young and old, wishing to try their skills can purchase a balsa wood airplane at the column's gift shop, climb the stairs, and launch their craft into the wild blue yonder. Will it make it all the way to the Washington side of the Columbia River...or just to the parking lot below?

The Astoria Column
1 Coxcomb Drive
Astoria, OR 97103
503-325-2963

- The Astoria Column is open from dawn to dusk.
- The Gift Shop is open Monday through Sunday – 9:00 a.m. to 7:00 p.m.
- There is no charge to visit the column, though parking is $5 per vehicle.

Driving Directions: From the Cannery Pier Hotel, proceed east on W. Marine Drive at the entrance to the hotel, and follow this as it turns south onto 8th Street. Turn left / east onto Niagara Ave. and follow this to 15th Street. Turn left / north here and then take the next right onto Coxcomb Dr. and follow this up to the Astoria Column. Note: You'll pass your next stop, the Flavel House Museum, as you make your way south on 8th St.

☐ **Next Stop:** Flavel House Museum

One of the finest examples of Queen Anne architecture in Oregon, as well as the Pacific Northwest, the 1886 Captain George Flavel House and surrounding grounds take up an entire lot at the corner of 8th and Duane Street. Impressive in its time, as well as today, this 11,600 square-foot 2½ story home welcomes visitors with an abundance of grand rooms, all expertly decorated with high-quality period-specific furnishings, amenities and wood work. Being a museum, tours are offered in which visitors can roam about the home while learning about Captain George Flavel, a Bar Pilot on the Columbia River and one of Astoria's most influential citizens during the late 1800s.

Tickets for tours are available in the carriage house, located at the corner of 7th & Exchange Streets, at the southwest corner of the lot. Here, visitors can also watch a short orientation video about the home before embarking on their tour.

Flavel House Museum
441 8th Street
Astoria, OR 97103
503-325-2203

Open Monday through Sunday – 11:00 a.m. to 4:00 p.m.

Driving Directions: From the Astoria Column, return the way you came, driving on Niagara Ave. back to 8th Street. Turn right / north onto 8th Street and follow this ½ mile to the large Flavel House at 441 8th Street.

www.Discover-Oregon.com

**Next Stop:** Oregon Film Museum

Oregon has been the filming location for many famous movies, and these are celebrated at the Oregon Film Museum. Housed in the old 1914 Clatsop County Jail, you'll find tributes to The Goonies, Animal House, One Flew Over the Cuckoo's Nest, The Shining, Paint Your Wagon, Stand by Me, and many others.

Oregon Film Museum
732 Duane Street
Astoria, OR 97103
503-325-2203

Hours & Admission:

- $6.00 Adults, $2.00 Children 6 – 17
- May – Sept.: Monday through Sunday – 10:00 a.m. to 5:00 p.m.
- Oct. - April: Monday through Sunday – 11:00 a.m. to 4:00 p.m.

Driving Directions: The Oregon Film Museum is directly across the street from the Flavel House Museum.

Next Stop: Heritage Museum

Housed in a charming 1904 building which used to serve as Astoria's City Hall, the Heritage Museum allows visitors to explore the rich history of Astoria and Clatsop County, with exhibits featuring Native Americans of this area, early Pioneers, the logging, fishing and canning industries that were so important to Astoria, and the immigrants that arrived to work the difficult jobs in the forests, canneries and at sea. In addition, visitors can learn about the construction of Highway 101 and the campaign to build the Astoria-Megler Bridge.

Heritage Museum
1618 Exchange Street
Astoria, OR 97103
503-338-4849

- Open Monday through Sunday – 10:00 a.m. to 5:00 p.m.

Driving Directions: From the Flavel House, drive south on 8th Street one block to Exchange Street. Turn left / east here and proceed approximately ½ mile to 1618 Exchange Street.

☐ **Next Stop:** Museum of Whimsy

An eclectic and artistic collection of items assembled within two floors of a neo-classic bank building from the 1920s. Stop in to discover the "curious, whimsical, and fantastic".

Museum of Whimsy
1215 Duane Street
Astoria, OR 97103
425-417-6512

- Admission: $ 5 Per person - $10 Per family
- Open Friday through Sunday – 11:00 a.m. to 5:00 p.m.

Driving Directions: From the Heritage Museum, drive north on 16th Street and then turn left / west onto Duane Street. Travel 3 blocks to the museum. Parking is available in the museum's private lot at 1303 Exchange Street.

☐ **Next Stop:** Fort Clatsop & Lewis and Clark NHP

Step back in time with a visit to a replica of Fort Clatsop, where Lewis and Clark, as part of the Corps of Discovery, spent the long and difficult winter of 1805 to 1806 before embarking on their return journey back east to St. Louis.

Lewis and Clark NHP
92343 Fort Clatsop Road
Astoria, OR 97103
503-861-2471

- Open daily 9:00 a.m. to 6:00 p.m. – Late June to September, 9:00 a.m. to 5:00 p.m. during the winter.

Driving Directions: From the Museum of Whimsy, drive north on 11th Street and turn left / west onto Marine Drive / E Columbia River Hwy 30. From here, follow this as it makes its way west and then southwest out of Astoria and automatically turns into the Oregon Coast Hwy 101. At 4.4 miles, turn left / south off of Hwy 101 and onto *Hwy 101 Business*. Follow the signs to Lewis & Clark National Park / Fort Clatsop in 11.7 miles.

 ☐ **Next Stop:** Fort Stevens State Park

Located at the mouth of the Columbia River is historic Fort Stevens. Initially built in 1865 to protect this important waterway from Confederate gun boats and the British Navy during the Civil War, it continued to serve in this role during the Spanish-American War, World War I and World War II.

Today, the shadows and stories of its past are preserved for visitors as part of a 4,300 acre State Park offering a military museum, massive concrete artillery gun batteries, historic structures, Civil War reenactments, and an information center. In addition, visitors will find an abundance of recreational activities, including camping, hiking, wildlife viewing, biking and more. A favorite among visitors is a walk out on the ocean shore, where they will discover the rusting skeletal remains of the Peter Iredale, a four-masted sailing ship that ran ashore in 1906.

Note that tours of Fort Stevens are available by contacting the Friends of Old Fort Stevens at 503-861-2000.

> Fort Stevens State Park
> 100 Peter Iredale Road
> Hammond, OR 97121
> 800-551-6949

- Open: Daily – 6:00 a.m. to 10:00 p.m.

Driving Directions: From Fort Clatsop, return to the intersection you used earlier to turn onto *Hwy 101 Business*. Proceed north across this intersection (Crossing Hwy 101) onto Marlin Ave. In 0.4 mile, turn left / west onto E Harbor Street / Warrenton-Astoria Highway and follow this 0.8 mile to a 4-way stop in Warrenton. From here, proceed northwest on Hwy 104 for 3.2 miles to Hammond, OR. Follow the signs from here to Fort Stevens.

☐ Next Stop: Seaside, Oregon

If you're looking for a busy seaside resort town filled with many fun and different boardwalk-like activities, then you're looking for Seaside, Oregon. Punctuated by a main drag that funnels cars to a turnaround on the prom overlooking a broad sandy beach that goes on forever, Seaside offers families a generous mix of seaside activities, including indoor bumper cars, go-carts, miniature golf, paddle boats, bike rentals for a ride on the sand, Oregon's largest arcade, the Seaside Aquarium, an indoor mall with a colorful carousel, corn dogs, cotton candy and over 100 flavors of an Oregon Coast favorite...salt water taffy!

Driving Directions: From any of the sites at Fort Stevens, return to Hwy 101 and continue south for approximately 11 miles to Seaside, Oregon.

☐ **Next Stop:** Seaside Historical Society Museum

Step inside the Seaside Historical Society Museum to learn about Seaside's history as a resort town beginning in the late 1800s, including its interesting historical attractions, its busy boardwalk, the industries of the area, the Seaside Railroad, and more. In addition, tour the Butterfield Cottage and its gardens, which accurately depict a Seaside cottage in the year of 1912.

Seaside Museum & Historical Society
570 Necanicum Dr.
Seaside, OR 97138
503-738-7065

- Open Monday through Sat. – 10:00 a.m. to 3:00 p.m.

☐ **Next Stop:** Seaside Helicopter Tours

Your road trip discovering Oregon's scenic backroads and byways now takes to the air! Choose from a selection of different helicopter tours to see Seaside, Cannon Beach and Oregon's north coast from high in the sky.

Seaside Helicopter, LLC.
2665 South Roosevelt Drive
85913 US-101
Seaside, OR 97138
503-440-4123

Tour of Seaside: $55 Per person (3 Seat minimum) – Cannon Beach: $119 (2 Seat minimum) – Reservations are not required.

Open: Monday through Sunday – 12:00 p.m. to 6:00 p.m. Memorial Day Weekend through October. Hours are weather dependent, and they're open other times of the year, as well, including Spring Break in March and occasionally in winter.

Driving Directions: Seaside Helicopter Tours is located right next to Hwy 101, ¼ mile south of Seaside.

 ☐ **Next Stop:** Ecola State Park

Found between Seaside and Cannon Beach is scenic Ecola State Park. Here, multiple trails offer stunning views of the Pacific Ocean, secluded coves, Cannon Beach, and the abandoned Tillamook Rock Lighthouse, located on a ½ acre of rock 1.2 miles out into the  ocean from Tillamook Head. Note that a $5 Day Use permit is required to park at Ecola State Park, and permits may be purchased at the fee station on the drive into the park.

Hikes:

- Ecola Point to Indian Beach Hike – 1.5 Miles – Easy
- Clatsop Loop Hike – 3 Miles – 700' gain – Easy
- Crescent Beach Hike – 3.6 Miles – 310' of elevation gain – Moderate

Driving Directions: From Seaside Helicopter Tours, travel south on Hwy 101 for 5.5 miles to the exit for Ecola State Park. Follow the exit to where it merges with Fir Street and then continue on Fir Street 0.1 mile to E. 5th Street. Turn right onto E. 5th Street and follow this 0.1 mile to Ecola State Park Road.

 Next Stop: Cannon Beach, Oregon

 Voted one of the World's 100 Most Beautiful Places by National Geographic, Cannon Beach is a charming seaside town filled with a collection of shops, boutiques, art galleries, bookstores, glass blowing studios, restaurants, quaint beach cottages and more. In addition, it offers a broad sandy beach for strolling, as well as iconic Haystack Rock. Rising 235 feet above the ocean waves, it is home to colorful Tufted Puffins, as well as other ocean birds, and offers access to fascinating tide pools at low tide. See Page 45 for additional details.

Driving Directions: From Ecola State Park, return the way you came on Ecola State Park Road back to E 5th Street and then Fir Street. Turn right / southwest onto Fir Street and follow this to where it curves right / west onto E 3rd Street. Then turn left / south onto N Spruce Street and follow this one short block to 3rd Street. Turn right / west here and follow this as it curves around to N Hemlock Street. Follow this into Cannon Beach.

Tonight's Lodging - The Cannon Beach Hotel

One of the oldest hotels on the Oregon coast, and chosen as the finest Bed and Breakfast in Cannon Beach by the Travel Channel, the 1914 Cannon Beach Hotel welcomes guests with luxurious accommodations, custom-designed furnishings and bedding, plush towels and robes, and best of all, fresh-baked cookies. Perfect after a day of exploring and sightseeing.

Guests of the hotel may choose rooms in one of four properties, each located within a couple of blocks of each other and just a short walk from the beach:

- **The Cannon Beach Hotel** – A historic New England style hotel with luxurious rooms designed with couples in mind – Children over 16 please.

- **The Hearthstone Inn** – An inn featuring a rustic and artisan-crafted sense, with stone fireplaces and warm wood furnishings. Child and pet friendly. One block to the beach.

- **McBee Cottages** – Built between 1927 and 1941, these quaint cottages offer cozy, family friendly lodgings in an ambiance of the 1940s. Most offer small gas fireplaces and kitchenettes, and all are child and pet friendly. One block to the beach.

- **The Courtyard** – Designed for couples or guests with children over 12, these modern luxurious rooms all face a quiet courtyard with a bubbling fountain. Gas fireplaces, large 2-person spa tubs, warm robes and more amenities await guests, including local salt water taffy on your nightstand.

- Check-in between 4:00 and 10:00 p.m.
- Check-in for all 4 properties at The Cannon Beach Hotel.
- Guests staying at either the Hotel or the Courtyard accommodations may enjoy a complimentary breakfast at the Cannon Beach Café – A Parisian style café located inside the Cannon Beach Hotel.

The Cannon Beach Hotel
1116 S. Hemlock Street
Cannon Beach, OR 97110
503-436-1392

Driving Directions: You'll find the Cannon Beach Hotel on your right as you proceed south on Hemlock Street.

Lodging Option #1: The Stephanie Inn

Stay right on the beach in the luxurious Stephanie Inn. Oceanside rooms offer commanding views of the Pacific Ocean and Haystack Rock, as well as Jacuzzi tubs, gas fireplaces, comfortable bath robes, microwaves, snack refrigerators and coffee makers. With the ocean within a stone's throw, you can pick up a lantern for an evening's walk on the beach, or check out a beach cruiser bicycle to see the coast in style.

- 41 Deluxe rooms
- Check-in starts at 4:00 p.m.
- Complimentary gourmet chef's breakfast buffet for guests of the Hotel or Courtyard accommodations
- Children must be 12 and over
- Smoke and pet free rooms
- Electric vehicle charging stations

The Stephanie Inn
2740 S. Pacific
Cannon Beach, OR 97110
855-977-2444
info@stephanieinn.com

Driving Directions: From Cannon Beach / The Cannon Beach Hotel, proceed south on S. Hemlock Street through the "S curves" for 1 mile to Matanuska Street. Turn right / west here and you'll find the Stephanie Inn on your left.

Lodging Option #2: The Ocean Lodge

With its premiere ocean front setting and grand lodge styling, The Ocean Lodge welcomes guests with a warm interior of massive Douglas Fir beams, a two-story wood burning fireplace, 1940s Craftsman accents and, best of all, fresh hot beverages and home-baked cookies!

The Ocean Lodge
2864 S Pacific Street
Cannon Beach, OR 97110
503-436-2241

Notes

Day Two

Cannon Beach to Tillamook

Yaquina Bay Lighthouse

DAY 2
CANNON BEACH TO TILLAMOOK

Day 2 – Date: / /

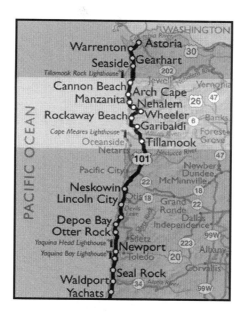

Summary: Where You're Going Today

- Cannon Beach, OR
- Oswald West State Park
- Wheeler, OR
- Rockaway Beach, OR
- Garibaldi, OR
- Tillamook, OR

Today takes you to a number of small Oregon Coast towns, where you'll explore a few different shops, discover a beautiful beach, see some surfers riding some waves, and set out to catch your own tasty Dungeness Crab for lunch. After your day of adventure and exploring, you'll arrive at the Sheltered Nook Tiny Homes, your unique destination for the day.

Tonight's Lodging:

- Sheltered Nook Tiny Homes

Today's Mileage: 58 Miles from Cannon Beach to Tillamook

Reservations Needed for This Segment:

- Sheltered Nook Tiny Homes – 503-805-5526 – 1 Night
- Oregon Coast Railriders - 541-786-6165
    - Departures at 9:00 a.m., 12:00 noon and 3:00 p.m.

Before You Leave:

 You may choose to fill your tank in Cannon Beach, though there will be other opportunities to get gas along the way.

Start

After exploring Cannon Beach this morning, travel south on Highway 101 and make your way towards your first prolonged stop of the day, the beautiful Oswald West State Park, where you'll enjoy a short hike to a very picturesque beach.

Note: Today's itinerary includes the opportunity to go crabbing for Dungeness crab at Kelly's Brighton Marina at the southern end of Nehalem Bay, either off a dock or from within a rental boat, and this will require 2 or 3 hours, depending upon which crabbing method you choose. (You can also just buy and eat a fresh-cooked crab at Kelly's, which will save time, if need be.) In addition, you'll have the opportunity to pedal a 12 mile section of the coast with the Oregon Coast Railriders, an experience that takes about 3 hours, and they depart at 9:00 a.m., 12:00 noon, and 3:00 p.m. You'll want to factor these two fun adventures into your timeline for the day.

☐ First Stop: Icefire Glassworks

Located across the street from The Cannon Beach Hotel is Icefire Glassworks, a working glass studio offering colorful works of glass art for sale, as well as close up views of glass artist James Kingwell skillfully practicing his craft.

Icefire Glassworks
116 E Gower Ave.
Cannon Beach, OR 97110
503-436-2359

- Open: Monday through Sunday – 10:00 a.m. to 5:00 p.m. – Closed Tuesdays and Wednesdays in the winter.

Driving Directions: Located across the street from the Cannon Beach Hotel.

☐ Next Stop: Haystack Rock

One of the most iconic landmarks in all of Oregon, Haystack Rock stands as a towering force against the tides and torrents of the Pacific Ocean. Rising 235 feet above the waves, it beckons tourists to explore its ever-changing tide pools and discover colorful sea stars, anemones, sea urchins, crabs and more, all as one of Oregon's seven designated Marine Gardens. High on its rocky perches, visitors will find an abundance of birdlife, including the Pelagic Cormorant, Black Oystercatcher,

Harlequin Ducks, the Pigeon Guillemot and colorful Tufted Puffins, which can be spotted during the early spring to mid-summer months, with the best times being early April to mid-May and late June through July.

Note:

- There are two Haystack Rocks on the coast. You'll see another during Day 3, when you visit Pacific City.

- To visit the tide pools, plan to arrive at Haystack Rock at least one hour before low tide. Weather and low tides permitting, you'll often find naturalists on the beach throughout the year offering a wealth of interpretive information about the tide pools, as well as the sea life and birds that inhabit the rock.

- Always practice beach safety when exploring the tide pools. Know if the tide is coming in or going out, and *never turn your back on the ocean*, as a large "sneaker wave" can come at any time to sweep you or a loved one from the rocks.

Directions: Walk almost any street heading west from Hemlock Street to reach the beach and walk to Haystack Rock.

☐ Next Stop: Cannon Beach History Center & Museum

Stop in at the Cannon Beach History Center & Museum to learn about the history of Cannon Beach and the interesting story of how the town got its name. In addition, take a moment to peruse through their interesting collection of over 12,000 historical photos.

Note: If you're visiting Cannon Beach during the second weekend in September, you can join the Cannon Beach History Center & Museum for its annual Cottage & Garden Tour, a self-guided and self-paced tour of the private homes and gardens of Cannon Beach. Maps are handed out at the start of the tour and are your ticket inside each home. Contact the Cannon Beach History Center and Museum for additional information at www.CBHistory.org

Cannon Beach History Center and Museum
1387 S. Spruce Street
Cannon Beach, OR 97110
503-436-9301

- Open Wednesday through Monday - 11:00 a.m. to 4:00 p.m.

Driving Directions: From the Cannon Beach Hotel, drive south on S. Hemlock Street for approximately 1 block and turn left / east onto Dawes Ave. Proceed 1 block and turn right / south onto S. Spruce Street, and then continue for about 1 block and you'll find the museum on your left.

Next Stop: Oswald West State Park – Hike to Short Sand Beach

Of the hikes we've done on the Oregon Coast, this one rates in the Top 10 for us. In fact, Kristy says it's one of her Top three favorite picnic spots on the entire coast, with the other two being at Cape Perpetua and the Umpqua Lighthouse.

Park in the large parking lot and take the trail at the north end of the lot under Hwy 101. (Watch your head!) Hike ½ mile on the broad and largely smooth trail to Short Sand Beach. Here, you can walk the short beach, explore a small (and short) cave on the north end at low tide, and watch surfers practice in the waves. Note: There are three picnic tables and three benches for enjoying the view. You'll find restrooms in the parking lot, as well.

Driving Directions: From the Cannon Beach History Center and Museum, proceed a short distance south on Spruce Street to Sunset Blvd. and turn left / east. Take the onramp to Hwy 101 marked "Nehalem, Rockaway, Tillamook" and proceed south from here 9.6 miles to the large paved parking lot for the Short Sands Trail – North Trailhead, on your left after crossing a small bridge.

☐ Next Stop: Nehalem, Oregon

 Spanning both sides of Hwy 101, Nehalem is a quaint beach town welcoming travelers to stop and visit. Take the time to peruse some shops, find an antique or two, and enjoy a treat at Buttercup Handmade Ice Cream and Chowders.

35915 N Hwy 101
Nehalem, OR 97131
503-368-2469

- Open Wednesday through Sunday – 11:30 a.m. to 6:00 p.m.

Driving Directions: From the Short Sands Trail – North Trailhead parking lot, proceed south on Hwy 101 for 6 miles to the town of Nehalem.

☐ **Next Stop:** Wheeler, Oregon

As with Nehalem, Wheeler, Oregon welcomes visitors with a small collection of shops. Take the time to stop in at the Old Wheeler Hotel, which has been very nicely renovated in period-specific detail, complete with three-pane windows, and ask if you may have a quick tour for future reference. We didn't stay here, but after touring it, we will in the future. You may want to consider this, as well as the Wheeler on the Bay Lodge and Resort across the street as alternatives to tonight's lodging, since they are only 22 miles north of Tillamook.

Old Wheeler Hotel
495 Hwy 101
Wheeler, OR 97147
503-368-6000

Driving Directions: From Nehalem, continue south on Hwy 101 for a little over 2 miles to Wheeler, OR.

 ☐ **Next Stop:** Kelly's Brighton Marina

You can't have the Oregon Coast without Dungeness crab, and you can't have Dungeness crab without going crabbing!

There are a number of places along the Oregon Coast where you can go crabbing, and we recommend two within this

49

guide. The first you'll come across is Kelly's Brighton Marina, just south of Wheeler, OR and Nehalem Bay. Bustling with families, campers, and road trippers on a summer's day, Kelly's Brighton Marina welcomes crabbers of all kinds, be they salty seasoned pros or novices visiting the ocean for their very first time. Kelly himself will see to it that you learn everything you need to know to catch, cook, clean and eat a crab, all while having fun doing it. In fact, he promises you'll have a blast!

If you haven't been crabbing before, here's the process...

- Rent some crab rings, bait, and a nice clean motorboat from Kelly's Brighton Marina. It's $110 for 2 hours and $25 for each additional hour. For this, you'll receive a boat and motor, 3 baited crab  rings, safety gear, and the cooking of any legal sized crabs you catch. (You *must* return any females or less than legal sized crabs to the water.)

- Head out into the bay (not the ocean!) and drop your crab rings into the water. Pull them up periodically to see what you've caught. Return to shore with your legal crabs and have Kelly's cook them up for you. Cooking the crabs takes 20 to 30 minutes.

- Clean your crabs and then find a picnic table outside Kelly's with a view of the bay and enjoy this delectable taste of Oregon with a plate, utensils and shell cracker provided as part of your boat rental fee.

As an option to renting a boat, you may rent a crab ring and crab off of Kelly's dock. For $15 you'll receive a crab ring with the first round of bait, access to the dock, and cooking of any legal sized crabs. The dock closes at 5:00 p.m. or one hour before dark, whichever is earlier.

Note: If you do not have an Oregon annual shellfish license, you'll need buy one here for $10.00.

Kelly's Brighton Marina
29200 US-101
Rockaway Beach, OR 97136
503-368-5745

- Open Monday through Sunday – 6:00 a.m. to 6:30 p.m.

Note: The second location we recommend for crabbing is at Tony's Crab Shack in Bandon, Oregon. See Page 148.

Driving Directions: From the town of Wheeler, drive south on Hwy 101 for approximately 3.5 miles to Kelly's Brighton Marina, on your right.

☐ Next Stop: International Police Museum

Stop in to see an interesting small museum dedicated to preserving the culture, history and heritage of the Rockaway Beach and Oregon police departments. You'll find many national and international departments represented here, as well.

International Police Museum
216 US-101
Rockaway Beach, OR 97136

- Open Monday through Friday – 10:00 a.m. to 4:00 p.m.

Driving Directions: From the marina, drive south on Hwy 101 for 4 miles to the town of Rockaway Beach, and park in the large public parking area on the right midway through town. Then simply walk back north a few blocks to the museum.

☐ Next Stop: The Original Pronto Pup

You've had them at carnivals, state fairs and ballgames, but did you know that corndogs were invented right here, in Rockaway Beach, Oregon? Stop in at the Original Pronto Pup and enjoy a taste of history. When you're finished, take a ride on the world's first Riding Mechanical Corndog, just outside the restaurant.

Pronto Pup
602 US-101
Rockaway Beach, OR 97136
971-306-1164

- Open Thursday through Saturday – 11:00 a.m. to 7:00 p.m., Sundays 11:00 a.m. to 4:00 p.m. – Closed Monday through Thursday from October until Memorial Day.

Driving Directions: From the public parking area, continue south on Hwy 101 for a little over ½ mile to The Pronto Pup.

☐ Next Stop: Garibaldi Maritime Museum

Stop in at the Garibaldi Maritime Museum to learn all about the voyages of Captain Robert Gray. Inside, you'll discover models of his ships, the Lady Washington and the Columbia Rediviva, as well as countless historical seafaring items including a partially completed 18th century transport boat, an eight foot tall reproduction of the Columbia's

figurehead, a half-model depicting how his ships were provisioned for long voyages to the Pacific Northwest, and much more. This is a very interesting and well-curated museum.

Admission:

- $4.00 – Visitors 11 and older
- $3.00 – Seniors 62 and over
- Children 10 and younger are free

Open:

- April through October: Thursday through Monday – 10:00 a.m. to 4:00 p.m.
- March *and* November: Weekends – 10:00 a.m. to 4:00 p.m.
- December, January and February: By Appointment

Garibaldi Maritime Museum
112 Garibaldi Ave.
Garibaldi, OR 97118
503-322-8411

Driving Directions: From the Pronto Pup, drive south on Hwy 101 for 4.5 miles to the large Garibaldi Museum on your left.

 Next Stop: Oregon Coast Railriders

A truly unique Oregon Coast adventure!

Sit down aboard a custom-built four-seater railrider and pedal 12 miles round-trip along an abandoned rail line from Bay City to Tillamook to experience the Oregon Coast like never

before. Being a former rail line, the grade is only ½ percent, so it's an adventure the entire family can enjoy, as well as nature enthusiasts, cyclists, birders, and of course, rail fans.

Note: Plan on arriving 30 minutes before your departure to sign in, be assigned a railcar, and load. Most round-trips take approximately 2 hours and 45 minutes total. Departures occur at 9:00 a.m., 12:00 noon and 3:00 p.m.

- There are two guides with each trip
- $26 Per person 12 years and older
- $16 per child 11 years and younger when accompanied by an adult – Car seats can be accommodated – Let them know of your need for a seat when making a reservation
- Each guest must weigh 250 lbs or less
- Pets are not allowed
- Please dress for the weather – OC Railriders usually rolls, rain or shine
- Open Thursday through Monday – 8:00 a.m. to 5:00 p.m.
- Closed early October until May
- Reservations are required – Reserve online at www.OCRailriders.com

Oregon Coast Railriders
5400 Hayes Oyster Drive
Bay City, OR 97107
541-786-6165
Info@OCRailriders.com

Driving Directions: From the Garibaldi Maritime Museum, proceed south on Hwy 101 for 4 miles to Hayes Oyster Drive. (Look for the huge pile of oyster shells here) Turn right / west here and immediately turn left into the parking area for the Oregon Coast Railriders.

Tillamook

☐ **Next Stop:** The Tillamook Creamery

No visit to Tillamook is complete without a visit to The Tillamook Creamery. A very popular Oregon icon, the factory itself and the Tillamook Cheese and Tillamook Ice Cream it produces are known statewide and around the world. Here, visitors take a self-guided tour through the newly remodeled state-of-the-art factory to see the entire cheese making process, from the arrival of fresh milk from the dairy farms surrounding Tillamook to the production of curds and whey, and finally the different cheese products enjoyed by so many. Be sure to stop in and see this popular family friendly attraction while in Tillamook, have some breakfast, lunch or dinner, and don't forget to enjoy some tasty ice cream before you go!

The Tillamook Creamery
4175 US-101
Tillamook, OR 97141
503-815-1300

- Open Monday through Sunday – 8:00 a.m. to 6:00 p.m.

Driving Directions: From the Oregon Coast Railriders, continue south on Hwy 101 for 3.7 miles to The Tillamook Creamery building on your left.

☐ **Next Stop:** Tillamook County Pioneer Museum

Located in the old courthouse building, the Tillamook County Pioneer Museum preserves the history of the Tillamook area, as well as the north coast, showcasing the early Native Americans of the region, explorers who arrived by ship and foot, pioneering families, early industries and more. In addition, the museum features an impressive collection of the region's wildlife, as well as a special room dedicated to Abraham Lincoln, which includes a rare document signed by the President.

Note: If you're looking for an interesting book about Tillamook, the north coast region, and the history of the area, be sure to check out the museum's abundant selection of books in their museum store.

Tillamook County Pioneer Museum
2106 2nd Street
Tillamook, OR 97141
503-842-4553

- Open Tuesday through Sunday – 10:00 a.m. to 4:00 p.m.

Driving Directions: From The Tillamook Creamery, drive south on Hwy 101 for 2 miles into Tillamook and turn left / east onto 3rd Street. Continue for 1 block and turn left / north onto what is now Hwy 101 North. Drive for 1 block north and turn right / east onto 2nd Street, where you'll find the museum.

☐ Next Stop: Tillamook Air Museum

The first thing that strikes you about the building for the Tillamook Air Museum, a former WWII era blimp hanger, is its immense size. Step inside, look up, and be amazed at this massive wooden structure. You've never seen anything like it. Nearby, you'll find perhaps a dozen or so rare and vintage aircraft parked within a large tent inside the hangar. Outside the tent, yet still inside the blimp hangar, is a collection of other vehicles, which changes from time to time and may include some vintage fire trucks, military vehicles, and even a steam engine being stored for the Oregon Coast Scenic Railroad.

Tillamook Air Museum
6030 Hangar Road
Tillamook, OR 97141
503-842-1130

- Open: Summer - Monday through Sunday – 10:00 a.m. to 5:00 p.m. – Closed on Mondays during the winter.

Driving Directions: From the museum, return to Hwy 101 south and proceed for 2.5 miles to Long Prairie Road. Turn left / east and follow the signs to the large hangar.

TONIGHT'S LODGING - SHELTERED NOOK TINY HOMES IN TILLAMOOK, OR

Discover the Oregon Coast's scenic backroads and byways by day, while staying in historic hotels by night.

OK, the Sheltered Nook Tiny Homes in Tillamook may not be a historic hotel, but they definitely are unique...and fun! Welcoming travelers with their small stature but big list of amenities, each of six themed tiny homes offer 385 square feet of living space, a Master Bedroom with a queen-sized bed, a sleeping loft with two queen-sized beds, a bathroom with a full-sized shower, a fully stocked kitchen with full-sized appliances, a small dining / living room area, Wi-Fi, a TV, and a front deck with a barbeque. In addition, finish the evening while enjoying s'mores around the fire pit out front, and when morning arrives, you'll be greeted with breakfast brought to your front door. Inquire about special dining needs when making your reservation.

Note: Each tiny home has a loft, which holds two queen beds. The ceiling is *low* up there, however. The kids will love it.

Sheltered Nook Tiny Homes
7860 Warren Street
Bay City, OR 97107
503-805-5526

Driving Directions: From the Tillamook Air Museum, return to Hwy 101 and then proceed north *through* Tillamook for 7.2 miles to Warren Street. Turn left here and continue a short distance to find the Sheltered Nook Tiny Homes on your right.

Lodging Option #1: The Old Wheeler Hotel

If tiny homes are not your thing, then you may wish to return 25 miles back north to the Old Wheeler Hotel, which you passed earlier today. Built in 1920, it conveys a cozy and historic ambiance with beautifully appointed rooms offering fine bed linens, thick towels, modern amenities, quiet three-paned windows, views of Nehalem Bay and more. While in town, browse Wheeler's antique stores, art galleries, gift shops and restaurants, or rent a boat and motor across the bay to the town of Nehalem for a fun Oregon Coast adventure!

Old Wheeler Hotel
495 Hwy 101
Wheeler, OR 97147
503-368-6000

Driving Directions: From the Tillamook Air Museum, return to Hwy 101 and then proceed north for 25 miles to Wheeler, OR and the Old Wheeler Hotel, which you saw earlier today.

Lodging Option #2: Wheeler on the Bay Lodge

Located across from the Old Wheeler Hotel and right on the shores of Nehalem Bay, the award-winning Wheeler on the Bay Lodge provides a taste of the Oregon coast with quaint clean rooms offering soft beds, deep spa tubs, microwaves, fireplaces and complimentary movies, coffee, tea and hot chocolate. Better yet, guests can enjoy the lodge's private dock and sit right on the bay or even rent a kayak for a little exploring.

Wheeler on the Bay
US Highway 101
580 Marine Drive
Wheeler, OR 97147
503-368-5858

Driving Directions: From the Tillamook Air Museum, return to Hwy 101 and then proceed north for 25 miles to Wheeler, OR and the Wheeler on the Bay Lodge, which is located across from the Old Wheeler Hotel.

www.Discover-Oregon.com

Notes

Day Three

Tillamook to Depoe Bay

Cape Meares Lighthouse

DAY 3
TILLAMOOK TO DEPOE BAY

Day 3 – Date: /   /

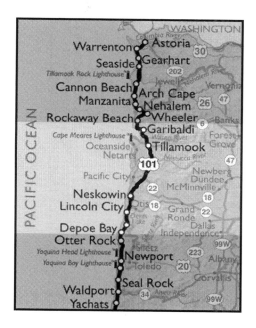

Summary: Where You're Going Today

- Garibaldi and Rockaway via the Oregon Coast Scenic Railroad
- Three Capes Scenic Drive
- Pacific City, OR
- Neskowin, OR
- Lincoln City, OR
- Depoe Bay, OR

Today begins with an exciting adventure aboard a 1925 steam locomotive, followed by an exploration of an amazing stretch of the Oregon Coast via the Three Capes Scenic Drive. Next, you'll visit the quaint beach town of Neskowin, (a favorite of ours) before continuing on to "busy" Lincoln City, where you may catch a colorful kite festival on the beach. Tonight, your journey ends at The Channel House in Depoe Bay, with its stunning view of the Pacific Ocean, complete with a passing whale or two.

Tonight's Lodging:

- The Channel House

Today's Mileage: 66 Miles from Garibaldi to Depoe Bay

Reservations Needed for This Segment:

- The Channel House – 541-765-2140 – 1 Night
- Oregon Coast Scenic Railroad – 503-842-7972
  Reservations aren't always necessary when riding in the "rolling stock" of the train, but if you'd like to ride in the locomotive cab, and we highly recommend you do, then its best to make reservations in advance.

Before You Leave:

Today involves a good deal of driving, so you may want to top off your tank in Tillamook.

Start

If you want to ride aboard a genuine 1925 steam train, then the start of your day will hinge upon catching the first train of the day from its station in Garibaldi, and this is at 10:00 a.m. Note that the station in Garibaldi is a little over 5 miles north on Hwy 101 from your Sheltered Nook tiny home, and this will take 10 to 15 minutes to travel.

If you'd prefer to skip the train, then feel free to begin your day on the Three Capes Scenic Drive, which begins on Page 67.

□ **First Stop:** The Oregon Coast Scenic Railroad

Journey back in time to the era of steam aboard the Oregon Coast Scenic Railroad. Climb aboard the vintage railcars, pulled by a massive 1925 steam locomotive, and journey north for 45 minutes from Garibaldi, OR to Rockaway Beach, OR. Along the way, you'll parallel Garibaldi Bay, ride along forested tracks, and pass through coastal neighborhoods before pulling into Rockaway, where you'll have 30 minutes to disembark and walk the nearby beach, explore some shops, and, of course, buy some saltwater taffy. Then, you'll reboard the steam train and enjoy your 45 minute return journey back to Garibaldi.

Note: For a truly unique Oregon Coast experience, make a reservation to ride in the cab of the locomotive for your round-trip journey. You'll get an up close look at the engine, be able to ask questions of the Engineer and Fireman, and, if you're lucky, actually pull the cord to blow the steam whistle! Make your reservations online before arriving.

Pricing:

Adults – 11 to 61 Years Old:	$22
Seniors – 62+ Years Old:	$20
Veterans – With Military ID:	$20
Children – 3 to 10 Years Old:	$15
Children Under 3 Years Old:	Free
Cab Rides – Per Person:	$72

Note: Tickets, once purchased, are non-refundable, but may be used to reschedule a similar excursion within the same year.

Tickets:

Tickets may be purchased in the caboose when you arrive at the station. Reservations for rides in the cab should be made online prior to your arrival, but may also be made after you arrive if space is available.

Schedule:

- Departing Garibaldi: 10:00 a.m., 12:00 p.m. & 2:00 p.m.

- Departing Rockaway Beach: 11:00 a.m. & 1:00 p.m.

Oregon Coast Scenic Railroad
402 American Avenue
Garibaldi, OR 97118
503-842-7972

Driving Directions: From the Tiny Nook Sheltered Homes, return to Hwy 101 and drive north for 5 miles to 3rd Street in Garibaldi. Turn left / south onto 3rd Street, cross the tracks, and then park on your right for the train.

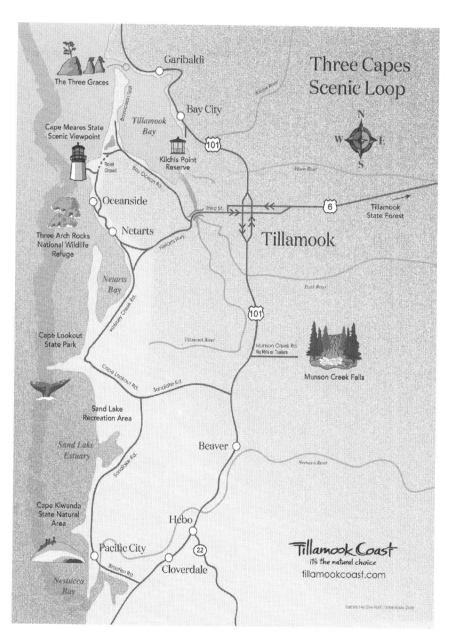

Map courtesy of www.TimberDoodleStudio.com

Three Capes Scenic Loop

Traveling from Tillamook to Pacific City, the Three Capes Scenic Loop is a 40 mile byway west of Hwy 101, which allows travelers to discover small ocean sidetowns, scenic coastal beaches and vistas, the beautiful Cape Meares Lighthouse, numerous historic sites, quaint shops and cafes, and three scenic capes; Cape Meares, Cape Lookout and Cape Kiwanda.

Driving Directions: From the Oregon Coast Scenic Railroad, return to Hwy 101 and proceed south for 9.9 miles to 3rd Street in Tillamook. Turn right / west onto 3rd Street, which will place you on 3rd Street / Highway 131. Follow this 1.8 miles to Bayocean Road NW, which leads to Cape Meares. Turn right here to begin the Three Capes Scenic Loop.

Important: Note that as of summer 2021, Bayocean Road NW does not extend counterclockwise to the Cape Meares Lighthouse due to a road closure. As a result, you'll need to skip turning onto Bayocean Road NW and instead continue past it on Highway 131 south and approach Cape Meares in a clockwise manner from the south, via Netarts and then Oceanside. See the map on the previous page, and follow the signs on the highway for Cape Meares via this "detour."

www.Discover-Oregon.com

☐ Three Capes Stop: Cape Meares State Park and the Cape Meares Lighthouse

Home to the shortest lighthouse in Oregon, commanding views, and the largest flocks of Murres in the United States, the Cape Meares Scenic Viewpoint and lighthouse offers plenty for its visitors. From the parking lot, walk the 0.2 mile paved downhill path to the short walkway above the lighthouse. From here, take in the scenic vista over the Pacific Ocean before descending down to the lighthouse itself. Join a free lighthouse tour anytime between 11:00 a.m. and 4:00 p.m. to see up close the lighthouse's impressive Fresnel lens and to learn about the history of the cape and its historic beacon. Afterwards, take the short trail south, which winds its way atop a towering cliff face with an amazing view to the ocean below, and take a moment to sit on one of the benches placed along the way. (The first one offers a better view than the second one.) Now return to the parking lot and cross it to find the 0.1 mile trail that leads to the interesting Octopus Tree and another beautiful view. Before you head back to your car, be sure to stop over at the viewing platform at the north end of the parking area for another impressive view.

Driving Directions: From the turn for Bayocean Road NW, continue northwest for 3.3 miles and turn left / south onto Bayshore Drive. Continue on Bayshore Drive for 2 miles to Cape Meares Lighthouse Drive. Turn right here and follow the signs to the parking for the lighthouse.

Three Capes Stop: Oceanside, Oregon

South of Cape Meares is the small quaint town of Oceanside, Oregon. Located at the ocean's edge, it lives up to its name, offering travelers a beautiful beach to stroll upon while taking in views of the sea stacks of the Three Arch Rocks National Wildlife Refuge just off shore.

Driving Directions: Return to Bayshore Drive and proceed south for 2.5 miles to Oceanside, where the scenic loop connects with the Netarts Oceanside Hwy W.

 Three Capes Stop: Netarts, Oregon

A quick right turn off of the Three Capes Scenic Loop will drop you right into the small town of Netarts, Oregon, located at the mouth of the 7 mile long Netarts Bay.

Driving Directions: From Oceanside, proceed south on the Three Capes Scenic Loop / Netarts Oceanside Hwy W. for 2 miles to Netarts.

 Three Capes Stop: Nevør Shellfish Farm

Located on Netarts Bay is the Nevør Shellfish Farm. Open to the public, it sells fresh Torkes, Kumamotos and Olympia oysters that have been sustainably grown and harvested in Netarts Bay, a natural environment that is immersed with sea water twice a day, leading to some of the freshest and most delicious oysters you've ever tasted. Stop in to pick up a dozen or two.

- Open Monday through Saturday – 10:00 a.m. to 5:00 p.m.

Nevør Shellfish Farm
6060 Whiskey Creek Rd.
Netarts Bay, OR 97141
503-812-5071

Driving Directions: From Netarts, drive to the south end of town and turn right onto Netarts Bay Drive. Follow this for 1.4 miles to where it connects with Whiskey Creek Road. Proceed south on Whiskey Creek Road (Still the Three Capes Scenic Loop) for 1 mile to the Nevør Shellfish Farm on the right.

 Three Capes Stop: Jacobsen Salt Company

Make your way down the narrow gravel roadway and find the small Jacobsen Salt Company, manufacturer of America's finest hand-harvested sea salt, which is made right on the bank of Netarts Bay. Inside the small gift shop, you'll find the very same gourmet salts they sell throughout Oregon and the world, including such flavors as Vanilla Bean, Lemon Zest, Pinot Noir, Smoked Cherrywood, Ghost Chili, Black Garlic and more. And yes, they're all salts! In addition, you'll find tasty confections, such as chocolates, black licorice, caramels and honey nut chews. You'll want to buy a gift pack for yourself and your favorite chef. Be sure to see the tiny salt crystals they have on display.

Jacobsen Salt Company
9820 Whiskey Creek Road
Tillamook, OR 97141
503-719-4973

- Open: Monday through Sunday – 10:00 a.m. to 5:00 p.m., December through February – 10:00 a.m. to 4:00 p.m.

Driving Directions: From the Nevør Shellfish Farm, continue south on Whiskey Creek Road for 1.8 miles to the Jacobsen Salt Company on the right. Proceed down the narrow driveway to the parking area.

 ☐ **Three Capes Stop:** Cape Lookout State Park

Jutting out into the ocean like a long straight-edged dagger, Cape Lookout is a cape like no other on the Oregon coast. Here, you'll find towering cliff faces rising more than 800' high along its two-mile length and offering dramatic views of the ocean below. And because  visitors are above the ocean instead of standing at sea level next to it, Cape Lookout is an excellent whale watching location, as it provides the unique perspective of looking down upon the whales from above, instead of out from the shoreline.

The cape also offers a few adventurous hikes. To see the captivating view at the tip of the cape, hike the Cape Trail.

Cape Trail – An easy to moderately difficult trail with interesting trees and numerous scenic viewpoints leads from the parking lot to the viewpoint at the tip of the cape. 2.4 Miles one way with 400' of elevation gain. Note that sections of the trail can be very muddy in wet weather, so wear appropriate footwear. Note, as well, that the tip of the cape, as well as numerous viewpoints along the trail, sit atop cliffs rising over 800' above the ocean, so be mindful of small children and pets.

Driving Directions: From the Jacobsen Salt Company, continue south on the Three Capes Scenic Loop for 3.7 miles to the parking for the Cape Lookout Trailhead on your right. Note that there are a couple of viewpoints of the cape along your drive, one of which is at the west end of the Cape Lookout State Park Campground, which you will pass at the 1.0 mile mark.

  ☐ **Three Capes Stop:** Pacific City and Cape Kiwanda State Park

If it's Oregon Coast adventure you're seeking, then you'll find it at active Pacific City. Here, visitors are welcomed with scenic views of Haystack Rock, a towering sand dune, Oregon's iconic dory boats, a beach they can drive upon, a short hike to beautiful Cape Kiwanda, and plenty of good food with a wide selection of beers.

Haystack Rock

Perhaps the first thing you notice when you pull into Pacific City from the north is impressive Haystack Rock, one of two towering sea stacks in the state sharing this name. Park for free in the large public parking lot opposite the Pelican Brewing Company, or drive down the large concrete ramp to park on the beach itself, which is an interesting experience. Note: Make sure the sand is not currently piled at the base of the ramp, as cars and trucks do get stuck here in the soft dry sand. Take note of the conditions at the base of the ramp, as well as the number of cars that have successfully driven and parked on the beach before making your way down. Park to the *south* of the ramp, as the area to the north is reserved for Dory fishermen.

Explore Cape Kiwanda

Now make your way towards the large sand dune that dominates the landscape to the north and hike the obvious trail making its way up and left towards the ocean. Once atop the plateau, you'll discover multiple overlooks offering views of yellow, orange and  rust colored sandstone cliffs carved into dramatic seascapes by the relentless ocean waves. Folks in the know make it a point to visit the cape during periods of heavy surf to watch spectacular displays of large waves exploding as they crash against the cliffs. *Cape Kiwanda photo © Shane Kucera*

The Large Sand Dune

 What's a trip to the Oregon Coast without gaining a summit? Return to the large sand dune and make your way to the top at 230' high. Your reward?...a speedy descent! Join your fellow sand hill enthusiasts and run full speed downhill to the base, filling your shoes with sand and your day with fun memories!

The Dory Fleet

 If you're lucky, you'll spot some dory boats from Oregon's iconic Dory Fleet both launching and coming ashore near the base of the giant sand hill. These small high-sided yet shallow draft boats with high bows actually launch and land in the surf. If

you see any dory boats in the vicinity, be sure to hang around and watch this Oregon Coast fishing tradition that reaches back over 115 years. *Photo courtesy of PacificCityFishing.com*

Pelican Brewing Company

You've had a busy afternoon, so head over to the Pelican Brewing Company near the parking area and enjoy some great food and a wide selection of excellent Oregon beers.

Dory Days

During mid-July of each year, Pacific City hosts Dory Days, a celebration of Oregon's unique Dory Boat fishing tradition, as well as the Oregon Coast lifestyle. Sponsored by the Pacific City-Nestucca Valley Chamber of Commerce and the Pacific City Dorymen's Association, visitors are welcome to enjoy a fun and colorful parade featuring decorated Dory Boats, live music, an artisan fair featuring local goods and crafts, kids activities, a hearty pancake breakfast and more.

Driving Directions: To reach the parking for Haystack Rock, Cape Kiwanda and the Pelican Brewing Company, continue south on Cape Lookout Road from the Cape Lookout Trailhead for 3.3 miles to Sandlake Road. Turn right / south here and continue on Sandlake Road for 6.4 miles to where it continues onto McPhillips Drive. Stay on McPhillips Drive for another 1.4 miles to the large parking area for the beach on your right.

The Grateful Bread Bakery

Step inside to find this small local bakery humming with activity. Enjoy breakfast, lunch, or dinner, as well as some of their freshly made breads and baked goods. Another one of our favorite places on the coast!

Grateful Bread Bakery
34805 Brooten Rd.
Cloverdale, OR 97112
503-965-7337

- Open: Thurs. through Mon. – 8:00 a.m. to 9:00 p.m. – Winter hours are 8:00 a.m. to 8:00 p.m. Closed mid-day.

Driving Directions: From the parking for Haystack Rock, drive south on Cape Kiwanda Drive (the main road south from the parking area) and proceed 1.0 mile to Pacific Avenue. Turn left and continue 0.2 mile across the bridge to Brooten Road and take a left here. Drive a few blocks to the bakery on your right.

☐ Next Stop: Neskowin, Oregon

Similar to Oceanside, Neskowin is a small beach town with a friendly neighborhood feel. Better yet, it offers a long beautiful stretch of beach, perfect for walking, which is anchored at its southern end by large Proposal Rock. Park your car at the parking area just off Hwy 101 and take the obvious path south of the lot, next to the creek, or walk west through the neighborhood streets to admire the quaint cottages and homes before reaching the beach. If you're anywhere near Neskowin during the 4th of July, then plan on spending the day here, as the whimsical morning parade is a joy, and the evening fireworks on the beach are not to be missed. Note: Many of the cottages are available for rent online.

Driving Directions: From the Grateful Bread Bakery, drive south on Brooten Road for 3 miles to Hwy 101, and then continue south on Hwy 101 for 6.5 miles to Hawk Street. Turn right / west here and park in the parking area.

☐ Next Stop: Cascade Head Preserve Hike & Viewpoint

The easy, short, and mostly level Nature Conservancy Trail takes hikers 1 mile through a beautiful coastal forest before reaching a grassy bluff offering one of the Oregon Coast's most iconic views, with the Pacific Ocean and the Salmon River Estuary far below. Keep an eye out for deer, elk, wildflowers, birds and butterflies.

Driving Directions: Return to Hwy 101 and proceed south for 3.5 miles to the turnoff on your right for the Cascade Head Preserve. Note that this turnoff is right at a crest in the road. Follow this well-maintained gravel road for 3.1 miles to the Nature Conservancy Trailhead. If you'd like to do some more hiking, you'll find the trailhead for the popular 2.7 mile Hart's Cove trail 1 mile further down the road.

☐ Next Stop: Drift Creek Covered Bridge

Oregon is home to a wealth of covered bridges, 54 of them, in fact! This next stop takes you a bit inland to discover Oregon's oldest covered bridge, the Drift Creek Covered Bridge. Built in 1914, this structure has quite a history. Destroyed by a flood in 1933, the bridge was rebuilt, but over time fell into a state of disrepair, eventually being scheduled by the State for demolition in 1997. However, local residents Kerry and Laura Sweitz offered to move the bridge to their property eight miles away, where they just happened to have a concrete bridge with the exact same dimensions. Through a lot of hard work on their part and other volunteers over the course of four years, the bridge was completely dismantled and then reassembled on the Sweitz's property, where it resides today.

Drift Creek Covered Bridge
1111 Bear Creek Road
Lincoln City, OR 97367

Note that as you drive to and from the Drift Creek Covered Bridge, you'll pass the small **Otis Café** on the north side of Hwy 18. If you're hungry, then this is an excellent place to grab a bite to eat.

Driving Directions: Return to Hwy 101 from the Nature Conservancy hike and drive south for 4.0 miles to the exit for Hwy 18 east. Travel on Hwy 18 east for 4.9 miles and turn right / south onto N Bear Creek Road / NF-17. Follow this for 0.9 mile to the bridge, which is on the left. Note: Park on Bear Creek Road and walk over to the bridge.

☐ Next Stop: Lincoln City

One of the most popular destinations on Oregon's "mid-coast", Lincoln City bustles with activity on any summer day. In addition to countless shops, a casino, a factory outlet mall and much more, Lincoln City is home to a seven

mile long beach which hosts a myriad activities, including the popular Lincoln City Summer Kite Festival in June, the Fall Kite

Festival in October, countless beach picnics, and an army of Float Fairies, who, as part of Lincoln City's "Finders Keepers" promotion, hide nearly 3,000 colorful glass floats between mid-October and Memorial Day each year anywhere along the seven mile shore, between the high tide line and the embankment. Since it's "finders keepers", if you find one, it's yours to keep!

Photo © Lincoln City Visitor & Convention Bureau

Driving Directions: Return to Hwy 101 via Hwy 18 and then continue south 4.5 miles to the large D River Beach Wayside. Turn right / west into the parking area at the stop light.

☐ Next Stop: Nelscott House Antiques

If you're a fan of Disneyana collectibles, then you'll like the Nelscott House Antiques shop. Stop in to see their amazing collection for sale, and be sure to ask about their rare "uranium glass" items from the 1930s. They glow in the dark!

Nelscott House Antiques
3200 US-101
Lincoln City, OR 97367
541-994-9761

- Open Monday through Saturday – 9:00 a.m. to 5:00 p.m., Sunday 10:00 a.m. to 5:00 p.m.

Driving Directions: From the D River Beach Wayside, travel south for 1.8 miles to Nelscott House Antiques on your left, immediately before the stop light.

TONIGHT'S LODGING -
THE CHANNEL HOUSE -
DEPOE BAY

Located on the channel to Depoe Bay, The Channel House welcomes visitors with 15 rooms and suites all within three separate buildings. After a day on the road, retire to your beautifully appointed room where you may enjoy the outdoor spa tub on your private deck as the sun reluctantly sinks below the horizon, casting a colorful sunset across your expansive ocean view. And if the weather is more wet than welcoming, then the gas fireplace inside is perfect for a cozy evening indoors.

If you've arrived early in the day, then walk over to "downtown" Depoe Bay, where you can enjoy the Depoe Bay Whale Watching Center, as well as explore shops filled with coastal souvenirs, antiques and artwork.

Note: Breakfast is included with your stay.

The Channel House
35 Ellingson Street
Depoe Bay, OR 97341
541-765-2140

Driving Directions: From Lincoln City, travel south for a little over 12 miles to Depoe Bay, Oregon. Turn right / west onto Ellingson Street immediately after crossing the bridge over the channel into Depoe Bay and you'll find The Channel House at the end of Ellingson Street, on your right.

Lodging Option: The Whale Cove Inn

Enjoy the modern comforts of a 4-Star hotel during your Oregon Coast road trip with a stay at the Whale Cove Inn. Located just south of Depoe Bay, its luxurious rooms and suites afford a sense of romance, pampering and privacy, all with impressive views of the Oregon Coast and Whale Cove Habitat Refuge.

Whale Cove Inn
2345 US-101
Depoe Bay, OR 97341
541-765-4300
www.WhaleCoveInn.com

Driving Directions: The Whale Cove Inn is a little less than 2 miles south of Depoe Bay on Hwy 101.

www.Discover-Oregon.com

Notes

Day Four

Depoe Bay
To Newport

Yaquina Head Lighthouse

DAY 4
DEPOE BAY TO NEWPORT

Day 4 – Date: /   /

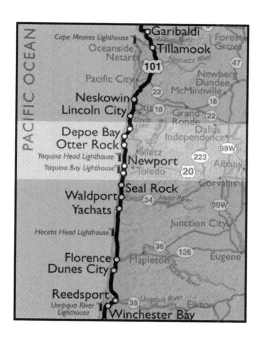

Summary: Where You're Going Today

- Depoe Bay, OR
- Yaquina Bay State Recreation Site
- Nye Beach, OR
- Newport, OR

You'll begin your day with an exciting "up close" whale watching tour on the Pacific Ocean before taking in the scenery (and tidepools) of the Yaquina Head State Recreation Site and Lighthouse. From here, you'll peruse some shops in Nye Beach, dial in on an old telephone museum, and visit a second historic Yaquina lighthouse before discovering Newport's busy waterfront.

Tonight's Lodging:

- The Sylvia Beach Hotel B & B

Today's Mileage: 13 Miles from Depoe Bay to Newport

Reservations Needed for This Segment:

- The Sylvia Beach Hotel B & B – 541-265-5428 - 1 Night
- Carrie's Whale Watching Tours – 541-912-6734

Start

Your morning begins with majestic gray whales. Walk across the bridge on the west side of Hwy 101 to the Depoe Bay Whale Watching Center to observe whales from land, or cross Hwy 101 at the light and visit Carrie's Whale Watching Tours to see them up close from a Zodiac boat on the ocean. Afterwards, make your way south to discover the Yaquina Head Lighthouse, Nye Beach and Newport, Oregon.

☐ First Stop: Depoe Bay Whale Watching Center

Located inside a building on the seawall overlooking the ocean in Depoe Bay, the Whale Watching Center is staffed with Oregon State Park personnel who are happy to answer your questions and help you spot some of the nearly 20,000 Gray Whales that migrate past the center each year on their way between Alaska and Mexico. Beginning with a surge in March and continuing through June, the Spring migration brings an abundance of whales making their way north to Alaska, while Summer and

Fall bring fewer migrating whales, but a pod of about 20 make their summer home just off Depoe Bay, where visitors can easily spot them spouting, spyhopping and diving.

Depoe Bay Whale Watching Center
119 US-101
Depoe Bay, OR 97341
541-765-3304

Open Monday through Sunday – 10:00 a.m. to 4:00 p.m. Closed Mondays and Tuesdays during the winter.

Directions: The Depoe Bay Whale Watching Center is across the *channel* from The Channel House. Simply walk across the bridge over the channel and you'll find the center on your left.

 ☐ **Next Stop:** Carrie's Whale Watching Tours & Whale, Sealife and Shark Museum

It's one thing to see glimpses of the majestic whales from land, but it is a dramatically different experience to see them from the water. Join Carrie Newell, a Marine Biologist with a PhD in Marine Biology, and her captains aboard a Zodiac for a 1.5 hour educational excursion on the ocean just off Depoe Bay. Here, you'll learn all about the many fascinating sea animals that inhabit Oregon's coastal waters, including the approximately 20 resident Gray Whales which spend their summer just offshore.

- Rates: $45 per person. Children 12 and under are $35. Children under 2 years of age are not allowed. Each trip is 1.5 hours, though 1 and 2 hour trips are also available. Inquire about these when booking your trip.

- Book your trip at 541-912-6734 or online (Recommended) at www.OregonWhales.com. Reservations for whale watching trips should be made 3 to 5 days in advance during the summer months. Call *the morning before* your departure to check weather conditions for the day of your trip. Check in at the museum ½ hour prior to your departure time.

- Departures are at 10:00 a.m., 12:00 p.m. and 2:00 p.m.

- Daily trips are scheduled according to the current ocean conditions, and your excursion will not go out in rough seas. There is little chance of getting sea sickness, and travelers seldom get wet. Note that temperatures on the ocean can be chilly, so dress accordingly. It's best to have jackets, hats and gloves available.

Carrie's Whale Watching Tours
234 US-101
Depoe Bay, OR 97341
541-912-6734

- Open Monday through Sunday – 10:00 a.m. to 4:00 p.m. – Winter Hours: 11:00 a.m. to 4:00 p.m.

Directions: Carrie's Whale Watching Tours is directly across Hwy 101 from The Channel House. You can cross Hwy 101 at the stop light north of the bridge over the channel.

Otter Crest Loop

As with the Three Capes Scenic Loop, the Charleston to Bandon Scenic Tour Route, and the Cape Arago Beach Loop, the 3.6 mile Otter Crest Loop steers travelers off of Hwy 101 for a slower paced journey along a more scenic section of the coast. Here, those who decide to explore will be rewarded with panoramic vistas, scenic viewpoints, intriguing coastal features and even a spouting whale or two!

You'll find the northern entrance to the Otter Crest Loop at approximately 2 miles south of Depoe Bay. (2.2 Miles from the bridge over Depoe Bay) Look for a small sign on your right that reads *Otter Crest Lp.* and veer off to your right here. Reset your odometer at this point. The road will reduce down to one lane for 1.2 miles at the 0.7 mile mark.

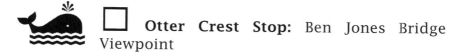 **Otter Crest Stop:** Ben Jones Bridge Viewpoint

Designed by Conde McCullough, who was the primary engineer of the many graceful bridges spanning the Oregon Coast Highway, the Ben Jones Bridge seen here is a tribute to the "Father of the Oregon Coast Highway", Ben Jones, the man who introduced legislation for the funding and construction of the highway in 1919.

At 0.3 miles after entering the Otter Crest Loop, look for a large paved pullout and viewing area on the right immediately after crossing the bridge.

 **Otter Crest Stop:** Cape Foulweather and Otter Crest State Scenic Viewpoint

Chances are both the weather and the view will be stunning when you stop by the Otter Crest State Scenic Viewpoint during your drive. However, back in March of 1778, the seas were rough, the winds fierce, and the skies were foul when Captain Cook first laid eyes on Oregon and named the cape just to the north for the conditions he and his crew were enduring that day, Cape Foulweather. You, on the other hand, can stand on a point 500' above the ocean and enjoy sunny skies, panoramic vistas, and if you keep an eye out, a passing Gray Whale!

At 1.8 miles, park in the large paved lot at the Otter Crest State Scenic Viewpoint and walk a short distance to the viewpoint, as well as the nearby Lookout Observatory and Gift Shop.

 **Otter Crest Stop:** Devil's Punchbowl State Natural Area

 Located in the small beach community of Otter Rock, OR, the Devil's Punchbowl is a unique Oregon Coast geologic feature. Here, a massive bowl in the rock with openings to the ocean fills with water during high tide and stormy seas to create a churning "punchbowl" of waves and foam. Travelers can walk within it during low tide, and the area is an excellent location for spotting whales.

Note: This area is also a favorite spot for surfers.

At 3.2 miles, turn right / west onto 1st Street and continue 0.4 miles to the parking area for Devil's Punchbowl.

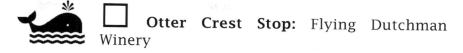 **Otter Crest Stop:** Flying Dutchman Winery

Located adjacent to the Devil's Punchbowl State Natural Area, the Flying Dutchman Winery is the only working winery on the Oregon Coast. Stop in to enjoy their award-winning wines in a wind-sheltered grove of shore pines offering a memorable ocean view. A gift shop offering just the right souvenir or wine-related gift is also available.

    Flying Dutchman Winery
    915 First Street
    Otter Rock, OR 97369
    541-765-2553

Located at the Devil's Punchbowl parking area.

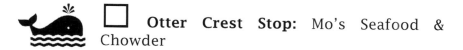 **Otter Crest Stop:** Mo's Seafood & Chowder

An Oregon Coast favorite since 1946, Mo's chowder is the perfect lunch or dinnertime treat, and it seems the more inclement the weather, the better the chowder! Stop in at the small Mo's Seafood & Chowder next to the Flying Dutchman Winery for a classic taste of the Oregon Coast!

    Mo's Seafood & Chowder
    122 First Street
    Otter Rock, OR 97369
    541-765-2442

Located at the Devil's Punchbowl parking area.

www.Discover-Oregon.com

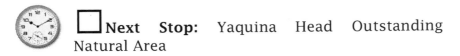 **Next Stop:** Yaquina Head Outstanding Natural Area

Standing majestically at the end of a mile long cape is the historic Yaquina Head Lighthouse. Oregon's tallest lighthouse at 93', this unwavering beacon has guided ships ashore and to safety for nearly 150 years. Today, travelers can take guided tours of the lighthouse, enjoy spotting whales as they migrate past the viewpoint, explore the nearby tide pools to find sea stars, crabs, sea anemones and more, and visit the nearby interpretive center to learn all about the history of the lighthouse and shipping off the Oregon coast.

45 Minute guided tours occur up to 12 times per day during the summer, and reservations are strongly recommended during the busy summer months. Winter tours occur more sporadically. Tickets are available on a first-come, first-served basis at the Interpretive Center on the day of your visit. Reservations may be made up to 90 days in advance during July through September by calling 1-877-444-6777 or visiting www.Recreation.gov. Note that space on the tours is limited.

The grounds open at 8:00 a.m. and close at sunset. There is a $7.00 per car entrance fee to the Natural Area.

By the way, Yaquina is pronounced "Yah Kwin Ah".

Yaquina Head Lighthouse & Interpretive Center
750 NW Lighthouse Drive
Newport, OR 97
541-574-3100

- Open: Monday through Friday – 10:00 a.m. to 4:00 p.m.

Driving Directions: Return on 1st Street to Otter Crest Loop and turn right. Continue south to Hwy 101. From here, drive south for 4.6 miles to NW Lighthouse Drive. Turn right / west here, at the stop light, and follow this past the fee station to the Interpretive Center and then the Yaquina Head Lighthouse.

☐ **Next Stop:** Historic Nye Beach

At the northern edge of Newport, OR, just a few blocks off of Hwy 101, is the small neighborhood of Nye Beach. Twelve blocks long and two blocks deep, it is filled with 40 locally owned businesses, including retail shops, restaurants, hotels, public parking, and more. It's a perfect area to get out of the car, explore and have some lunch. Note: Stroll to the beach, where you'll find a nice view of the Yaquina Head Lighthouse.

Driving Directions: Return to Hwy 101 and travel south for 2.6 miles to NW 3rd Street. Turn right / west here and continue 0.4 mile to NW Coast Street. Turn right / north and you'll be in the heart of historic Nye Beach.

Note: If you continue straight on 3rd Street and do not turn onto NW Coast Street, you'll arrive at the Sylvia Beach Hotel, where you'll be staying this evening. If your timing works out, you may wish to check in and drop off your bags before exploring Nye Beach and Newport.

☐ **Next Stop:** The Olde Telephone Company

 Step through the front door of the Olde Telephone Company and find hundreds of museum-quality antique phones, phone booths, signs, switchboards, and other phone-related paraphernalia on display. Then discover that everything you see is for sale! It's definitely unique and one of the most interesting "museums" on the coast.

> The Olde Telephone Company
> 255 SW 9th Street
> Newport, OR 97365
> 541-272-5225

- Open: Monday through Sunday – 10:00 a.m. to 5:00 p.m.

Driving Directions: From the corner of NW 3rd Street and NW Coast Street, head south on SW Coast Street for 0.6 mile to SW 2nd Street. Turn left / east here and follow this to SW Angle Street. Turn right onto SW Angle and cross Hwy 101. After 1 block, turn right / west onto SW 9th Street and find The Old Telephone Company on your left.

☐ Next Stop: Yaquina Bay Lighthouse

While the Yaquina Head Lighthouse stands as a tall sentinel at the northern end of Newport, the older Yaquina Bay Lighthouse resides in a small house at the south end of town and guides ships to a long jetty which leads them to Yaquina Bay.

Built atop a bluff at the mouth of the Yaquina River in 1871 and decommissioned only a few years later, in 1874, the Yaquina Bay Lighthouse is believed to be the oldest structure in Newport, and is the only historic wooden lighthouse still standing in Oregon.

Tour the lighthouse and its attached living quarters to see different rooms furnished just as they were in 1871, and make a point to go down to the basement where you can watch a short but interesting video about the lighthouse and its history. Tours are free, but donations are appreciated.

> Yaquina Bay Lighthouse & State Recreation Site
> Newport, OR 97365
> 541-265-5679

Lighthouse Hours:

- Monday through Friday – 10:00 a.m. to 4:00 p.m. - Memorial Day Weekend through the end of September.

- Monday through Friday – 12:00 p.m. to 4:00 p.m. – October to Memorial Day Weekend

Driving Directions: Return to Hwy 101 and drive south for 0.7 mile to the exit for the Yaquina Bay State Park. Take this and proceed west to the parking area for the lighthouse.

☐ Next Stop: Newport's Historic Bayfront

Walk along Newport's bustling bayfront and you'll see a collection of retail shops, restaurants, chowder houses, and other tourist attractions, but don't think for a moment that it's not a working commercial bayfront first and foremost. Home to Oregon's largest commercial fishing fleet and a corresponding collection of large seafood processing plants, you'll see forklifts hoisting large pallets of fish on ice next to the small shop selling t-shirts extolling Oregon's coastal life. A bit rough and unkept around the edges, just as it should be, the bayfront offers a wide collection of sites, sounds and smells. Stop and have some lunch at Mo's, walk the docks to see trawlers returning with their catch, mosey over to the loud barking sea lions making a commotion, or rent a crab ring and toss it over a dock railing to try your hand at tricking a large Dungeness crab into taking the bait.

Park your car along the main boulevard or find a public parking spot and walk the bayfront.

> Newport Historic Bayfront
> 250 – 300 SW Bay Blvd.
> Newport, OR 97365

Driving Directions: From the lighthouse, return towards Hwy 101, but do not access it. Instead, pass beneath it before turning right / east onto SW Naterlin Drive. Proceed on this for 1 block and then turn right onto SW Bay Blvd., which takes you to the bayfront.

☐ **Next Stop:** Marine Discovery Tours

Give up your role of landlubber and hop aboard Marine Discovery Tours' 65' Discovery cruise vessel for a two-hour educational tour. Narrated by friendly naturalist guides, this hands-on tour searches for...and usually finds...gray whales, harbor seals, porpoises, sea lions, bald eagles, pelicans and more. In addition, you'll get to touch a variety of sea life, including Dungeness and Rock crab, sea stars, and whatever else is brought up out of the ocean depths.

The tour makes its way out onto the ocean, where you'll see the Oregon coastline from an all new perspective, as well as two lighthouses, Newport's impressive jetty, and Oregon's largest commercial fishing fleet within Yaquina Bay. If ocean conditions are rough, then the heated Discovery will explore the 6 miles of Yaquina Bay and the Yaquina River.

Sea Life and Whale Watching tours operate daily from March through October. *Photo © Marine Discovery Cruise*

Marine Discovery Tours
345 SW Bay Blvd.
Newport, OR 97365
541-265-6200

- Summer Hours: Monday through Sunday – 10:00 a.m. to 6:00 p.m. Opening and closing hours can vary each day.

- Winter Hours: Monday through Sunday – 10:00 a.m. to 5:00 p.m.

Driving Directions: You'll find Marine Discovery Tours along the bayfront, across from SW Hurbert Street.

Next Stop: Oregon Coast Aquarium

Offering a world-class facility along Yaquina Bay, across from the historic waterfront, the Oregon Coast Aquarium is one of Oregon's top tourist attractions. Here, visitors can wander 23 acres to discover playful Sea Otters, an inquisitive Giant Pacific Octopus, colorful ocean birds, mesmerizing Jelly Fish, acrobatic Harbor Seals and Sea Lions, and much more, all as part of a marine educational attraction.

Plan on visiting for 1.5 to 2 hours. Free car and RV parking is available, and you'll also find the Ferry Slip Café, a coffee bar and a large gift shop. One third of the exhibits are outdoors, so dress accordingly. Pets are not allowed past the front gates.

Oregon Coast Aquarium
2820 SE Ferry Slip Road
Newport, OR 97365
541-867-3474

- Open Monday through Sunday – 10:00 a.m. to 5:00 p.m.

Admission:

Adult: (18 – 64)	$24.95
Senior: (65 +)	$19.95
Young Adult: (13 – 17)	$19.95
Child: (3 – 12)	$14.95

Driving Directions: Return back towards the Yaquina Bay Lighthouse, passing beneath Hwy 101 before accessing it southbound. Continue south across the Yaquina Bay Bridge and, shortly after crossing the bridge, take the exit right for the

Oregon Coast Aquarium. (SW Abalone Street) Follow this around and back north to where it turns into SE Marine Science Drive heading east. Turn right / south onto SE Ferry Slip Road and then take a left after 1 block into the entrance for the Oregon Coast Aquarium.

☐ Next Stop: Hatfield Marine Science Center

A working research lab, the Hatfield Marine Science Center studies and shares information on tsunamis, coastal erosion, sustainable fisheries, aquatic ecosystems and much more. In addition to its research, it operates an interpretive center, which is open to the public. Here, you can learn about the ocean environment through interesting displays and experience Tidepool Touch Tanks, where you can touch sea stars, sea urchins, abalone, anemones and other creatures found in the nearby coastal waters. If your timing is right, you may even be greeted by a Giant Pacific Octopus as you enter the exhibit area! Admission is free, but a suggested donation of $5 per person or $20 per family is appreciated.

Hatfield Marine Science Center
2030 SE Marine Science Drive
Newport, OR 97365
541-867-0100

- Summer Hours: Monday through Sunday - 10:00 a.m. to 5:00 p.m. - Memorial Day to Labor Day

- Winter Hours: Thursday through Monday - 10:00 a.m. to 4:00 p.m. - Labor Day to Memorial Day

Driving Directions: Return to SE Marine Science Drive and turn right / east. Follow this 0.4 mile to the Hatfield Marine Science Center, east of the roundabout.

TONIGHT'S LODGING - SYLVIA BEACH HOTEL B & B NEWPORT, OR

Walk into the charming 1912 Sylvia Beach Hotel and you'll instantly discover it is "truly a hotel for book lovers". Named after Sylvia Beach, the expatriate American bookseller and publisher who opened the small Shakespeare and Company bookstore in Paris, France, each of its 21 rooms are themed after a famous author, including Hemingway, F. Scott

Fitzgerald, Emily Dickinson, Mark Twain, J.K. Rowling and even Dr. Seuss. We've found it's the perfect location for getting out and exploring, but it's also just what you want for hunkering down with a good book and a cup of hot chocolate during...a dark and stormy night.

According to the hotel... *There are no telephones, TVs, or WiFi in rooms at the Sylvia Beach Hotel. The allure is beach quiet. Unplug, unwind, and sleep with your favorite author.*

Breakfast, including house made pastries, fresh fruit, juices, and cereals, pancakes and delectable entrees, is served each morning from 8:30 a.m. to 10:00 a.m. This is included in the price of your stay.

>Sylvia Beach Hotel B & B
>267 NW Cliff Street
>Newport, OR 97365
>541-265-5428
>www.SylviaBeachHotel.com

Driving Directions: Return to Nye Beach, where you'll find the Sylvia Beach Hotel at the end of NW 3rd Street.

Lodging Option: Ocean House Bed & Breakfast

What began as a two story beach cottage in 1937 is now a remodeled bed and breakfast, welcoming weary travelers with king and queen-sized beds, well-appointed rooms, modern day amenities, a full breakfast, and complimentary wine and fresh baked cookies.  Perched high on a forested bluff above Agate Beach in northern Newport, the Ocean House offers 7 rooms, six of which have beautiful ocean views.

>Ocean House Bed & Breakfast
>4920 NW Woody Way
>Newport, OR 97365
>541-265-3888

Notes

Day Five

Newport to Heceta Head

Heceta Head Lighthouse

DAY 5
NEWPORT TO HECETA HEAD

Day 5 – Date: /   /

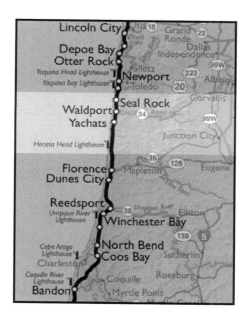

Summary: Where You're Going Today

Pacific Coast Scenic Byway

- Seal Rock State Recreation Site
- Yachats, OR
- Cape Perpetua
- Heceta Head

What awaits you today is one of the most dramatic sections of shoreline found on the Oregon Coast. You'll experience Devil's Churn, Thor's Well, Cook's Chasm, and the Spouting Horn before driving up to the historic Cape Perpetua Lookout, which offers a stunning panoramic view from 800' above the ocean. Your day won't end there, however, as you'll then be off to see...and stay at...the most photographed lighthouse on the Oregon Coast, Heceta Head.

Tonight's Lodging:

- Heceta Head Lighthouse Bed & Breakfast

Today's Mileage: 38 Miles from Newport to Heceta Head

Reservations Needed for This Segment:

- Heceta Head Lighthouse Bed & Breakfast – 541-547-3696
  – Make a reservation for 1 night

Start

Turn south onto Hwy 101, travel through Newport, and make your way to your first stop at the Ocean Beaches Glassblowing Gallery or Seal Rock State Recreation Site. Note: If you can last, we recommend you have only a light breakfast in Newport, and save your hunger for a "real" breakfast at the Drift Inn Hotel & Restaurant in Yachats, OR, your 3rd or 4th stop of the day.

Before You Leave:

Check your gas in Newport before you begin.

☐ First Stop: Ocean Beaches Glassblowing Gallery

In addition to seeing beautiful hand blown glass floats, ornaments, lamp shades, artwork and more, visitors to the Ocean Beaches Glassblowing Gallery can make their way towards the back where they can watch the glass blowing process almost every *afternoon* and ask questions.

106

Ocean Beaches Glassblowing Gallery
11175 US-101
Seal Rock, OR 97376
541-563-8632

- Summer: Mon. through Sun. – 9:00 a.m. to 6:00 p.m.
- Winter: Mon. through Thurs. – 10:00 a.m. to 6:00 p.m., Friday through Sunday – 9:00 a.m. to 6:00 p.m.

Driving Directions: From the Sylvia Beach Hotel, travel south on Hwy 101 for 10 miles to the gallery on your left.

☐ Next Stop: Seal Rock State Recreation Site

Seal Rock offers a beautiful view of the ocean, as well as seals, sea lions, birds and other marine life. You'll find beach access with tidepools to the south of the parking lot.

Seal Rock State Recreation Site
10032 NW Hwy 101
Seal Rock, OR 97376

Driving Directions: From the Ocean Beaches Glassblowing Gallery, proceed south on Hwy 101 for 0.6 mile to the parking area for Seal Rock State Recreation Site, on your right.

☐ Next Stop: Waldport Heritage Museum

Located in a former camp barracks built by the Civilian Conservation Corp in 1941, the Waldport Heritage Museum today offers an interesting collection of items reflecting the history of Waldport, OR and the surrounding area.

Admission is free, but donations are gladly accepted.

Waldport Heritage Museum
320 Northeast Grant Street
Waldport, OR 97394
541-563-7092

- Open: Thursday through Sunday – 12:00 p.m. to 4:00 p.m. (10:00 a.m. to 4:00 p.m. on Saturdays)

Note: If you continue north past the museum on NE Broadway Street, you'll eventually reach the Alsea River. Here you'll find parking and a busy dock area offering crab ring rentals. Popular with locals, these waters hold only Dungeness crab. No "lowly" rock crabs can be found here.

Driving Directions: From the Seal Rock State Recreation Site, travel south on Hwy 101 into Waldport and turn left / east at 5.0 miles onto NW Hemlock Street, at the light. Proceed east on NW Hemlock and then turn left / north onto NE Broadway Street. Continue north for 3 blocks to find the museum on your right, at the corner of Broadway and Grant.

☐ Next Stop: The Drift Inn & Cafe

For breakfast, you'll be eating at a place with décor that's as eclectic and flavorful as the menu. Stop at the historic and award-winning Drift Inn & Cafe, right on the edge of Hwy 101, and step inside for an tasty meal of breakfast favorites served by nice folks. While enjoying your cinnamon roll, be sure to read all about the inn's colorful and rowdy history on the back of the menu. Afterwards, take the time to walk out the end of the entrance hallway and explore a bit around the "campus" of buildings that make up the inn.

The Drift Inn & Cafe
124 US-101
Yachats, OR 97498
541-547-4477

- Open for breakfast, lunch and dinner
- Open Monday through Sunday – Summer: 8:00 a.m. to 10:00 p.m. – Winter: 8:00 a.m. to 9:00 p.m.

Driving Directions: From the Waldport Heritage Museum, return to Hwy 101 and proceed south for 8.5 miles, where you'll find the Drift Inn & Café on your left as you drive through Yachats.

☐ Next Stop: Little Log Church and Museum

It's not often you'll find a museum within a church, but you'll find one in Yachats at the Little Log Church by the Sea. Built in the shape of a cross, this small church was dedicated in 1930, but with its congregation moving to a larger church in 1969, it is  today operated as a museum by the Oregon Historical Society. Inside, you'll find the church lovingly preserved along with an interesting collection of items from Yachats' history. The museum is free, but donations are gladly accepted.

Little Log Church Museum
328 W 3rd Street
Yachats, OR 97498
541-547-4547

Driving Directions: From the Drift Inn & Café, return *north* on Hwy 101 only a couple of blocks and turn left / west onto 3rd Street. You'll spot the Little Log Church and Museum on your left, on the corner of 3rd and Pontiac Street.

Cape Perpetua Scenic Area

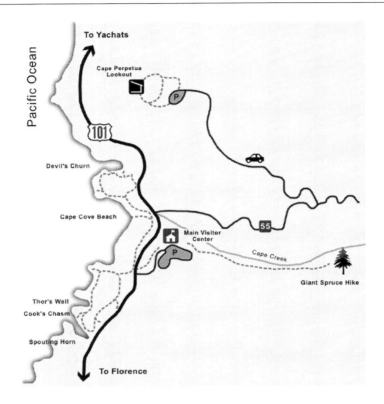

Cape Perpetua is a must-stop-and-see destination during your road trip. Geologic wonders, stunning ocean views, an enclosed whale watching facility, a bit of history, and just a touch of danger await at this highlight of the Oregon coast.

Note: Much of Cape Perpetua can be seen with a short stroll, but to see Devil's Churn, Cook's Chasm, Thor's Well, Spouting Horn, the historic CCC structure, and more up close, you'll need to hike a couple of interesting miles.

Driving Directions: The Cape Perpetua Scenic Area includes a couple of stops along Hwy 101, with the largest being at the main visitor center. If you plan on hiking today, we recommend that you do not stop at the Devil's Churn Scenic Overlook, (2.6 Miles from Yachats, OR) as parking is somewhat limited. Instead, proceed to the main Cape Perpetua Visitor Center (a short distance further south) and walk back north to see Devil's Churn up close. If you do not plan on hiking, then by all means stop at the Devil's Churn overlook and see this interesting Oregon feature.

☐ Cape Perpetua Stop: Main Visitor Center

A short walk from the parking area takes you to the main Cape Perpetua Visitor Center, where you can watch for whales in a park-like setting high above the ocean. Inside the Visitor Center, you'll find interpretive displays, as well as large viewing windows equipped with binoculars for spotting passing Gray Whales. Numerous paved trails from the Visitor Center lead to the features below, as well as viewing platforms and viewpoints overlooking the ocean.

Directions: From Yachats, drive south on Hwy 101 for 3.0 miles to the turnoff for the Main Visitor Center parking area.

☐ Cape Perpetua Stop: Devil's Churn

You'll find hiking maps for your next few stops at the Main Visitor Center. From here, follow a trail north to the overlook above Devil's Churn and see how this feature got its name. Afterwards, either make your way back to the Main Visitor Center and then  follow the trail towards the tidepools, Thor's Well, the Spouting Horn, and Cook's Chasm, or, *provided ocean conditions allow*, descend the trail at Devil's Churn towards the beach and then make your way south to these attractions on the sand and rock. Note: The tidepools are marginal, as we found mostly sea anemones and mussels.

Note: Ask at the Visitor Center today when high tide will be and make a note of this, since you'll have the opportunity to walk on the beach and stand near Thor's Well and Cook's Chasm, which are very close to the ocean waves.

☐ Cape Perpetua Stop: Thor's Well

We found Thor's Well to be a captivating highlight of the trip. Located at the water's edge is a large gaping barnacle and mussel encrusted hole perhaps 20' across that violently fills with water with each crashing wave from the ocean. Shooting through an opening at its base, the water instantly fills the well and often splashes over the top in dramatic fashion, only to quickly flush back out. It's a truly unique feature of the Oregon Coast.

Note: There is no railing or viewing platform here, and Thor's Well begs you to come closer to get that great photo, but one could easily be swept into the well with no warning, so be mindful of the distance you and little ones keep from it.

☐ Cape Perpetua Stop: Cook's Chasm

As with Devil's Churn, though on a smaller scale, waves roll into Cook's Chasm from the sea, creating an ever-roiling display of churning and splashing water.

☐ Cape Perpetua Stop: Spouting Horn

Like Thor's Well, the Spouting Horn is located within the rock right at the water's edge, and with just the right wave action, water rushes into the "horn" and sprays high into the air.

☐ Cape Perpetua Stop: 1933 CCC Lookout Shelter Atop Cape Perpetua

High above the Visitor Center, atop Cape Perpetua, is the West Shelter, a small stone structure built by the Civilian Conservation Corps. Standing 800' above the ocean, it holds a

commanding view of over 100 miles of coastline, as well as looks out over 37 miles to the horizon. Built in the summer of 1933, today it is a popular location for picnicking, whale watching, and getting married.

Note: If the weather is agreeable, the south facing slope atop Cape Perpetua is *the* perfect spot to sit down and enjoy lunch with a commanding view.

Driving Directions: From the Cape Perpetua Visitor Center, return to Hwy 101 and drive back *north* for 0.3 mile to road NFD-55, which leads to the Cape Perpetua Day Use Campground. Turn right / east here and proceed 0.8 mile to Cape Perpetua Lookout Road. Turn left here and follow this 0.9 mile to the Cape Perpetua Lookout parking area. Be sure to take the pathway to the south to see the amazing view and then wind your way north to find the CCC shelter.

☐ Next Stop: Heceta Head Lighthouse & Viewpoint

Your day finishes with a stop at one of the most beautiful and most photographed lighthouses in the world. Perched out on Heceta Head is the majestic Heceta Head Lighthouse. With a history reaching back to 1894, it still dutifully performs its task today, guiding ships to safety along the Oregon Coast.

Make your way along a trail from the parking area out to the lighthouse and its scenic viewpoint, where you may take a tour to learn about the history of the lighthouse, its construction, and its role today on the Oregon Coast. In addition, be sure to take the trail that leads near the Heceta Head Lighthouse Keeper's House, a restored 1893 home, which today serves as a bed and breakfast. (See Page 117) As a bed and breakfast, it is not open to the public.

- Stop at the Heceta Head Lighthouse at the end of today, or, if you're not staying at the historic Lighthouse Keeper's House this evening, then make it your first stop tomorrow, on Day 6.

- Lighthouse tours are given seven days a week, from 11:00 a.m. to 3:00 p.m. Tours are given until only 2:00 p.m. during the winter, weather and staff permitting.

- To capture a photo of the lighthouse from above, take the short trail which leads up the hill behind the lighthouse to a small viewpoint.

- Day-use parking permits ($5) are required at Heceta Head Lighthouse State Scenic Viewpoint and may be purchased from a machine at the park.

- For a dramatic and scenic view of the lighthouse, be sure to stop at the pullout located a little over one mile south of the lighthouse on Hwy 101.

Driving Directions If You **ARE** Staying This Evening at the Heceta Head Lighthouse Bed & Breakfast:

From the Cape Perpetua Lookout, return to Hwy 101. From here, travel south for 11.0 miles to Summer Street, the "guests only" road for parking at the Heceta Head Lighthouse B & B. Turn right here off of Hwy 101 and follow this to the parking for the B & B. Note: Summer Street IS NOT the paved road to the main Heceta Head Lighthouse parking area, which the public uses, but instead a small gravel road leading right off of Hwy 101 shortly after Mile Marker 178 and just before the paved road to the Heceta Head Lighthouse parking area. Summer Street tends to come up quickly on a rightward bend, so slow a bit and be looking for it.

Driving Directions If You **ARE NOT** Staying at the Heceta Head Lighthouse Bed & Breakfast:

From the Cape Perpetua Lookout, return to Hwy 101. From here, travel south for 11.1 miles to the exit for the parking area for the Heceta Head Lighthouse, on your right. Take this exit and make your way to the parking area.

Important! If you are leaving the Heceta Head Lighthouse Bed & Breakfast from Summer Street and wish to return *north* on Hwy 101, instead of south, DO NOT attempt to turn left and cross Hwy 101 on this somewhat blind curve, but instead turn right, drive south a short distance, and take the exit for the Heceta Head Lighthouse parking area. Then pass east and *underneath Hwy 101* so you can approach the highway from the other side and safely pull out northbound with an easy right turn.

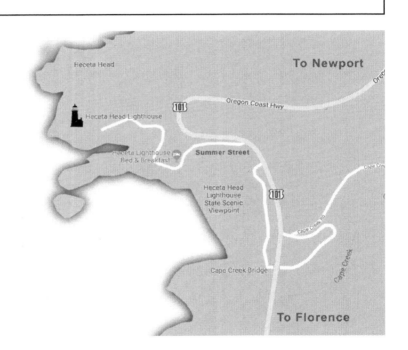

TONIGHT'S LODGING - HECETA HEAD LIGHTHOUSE BED & BREAKFAST

Standing majestically upon Heceta Head is the Heceta Head Lighthouse, recognized as one of the most beautiful lighthouses in the world. Built in 1894, its powerful beacon still shines today, casting its beam 21 miles out to sea, thus making it the brightest light on the Oregon Coast.

Perched high on a cliff only a short stroll inland is the historic Heceta Head Lighthouse Keeper's House. Owned by the Oregon State Parks division, this stately home is managed as a fine bed and breakfast, offering seven rooms, private baths, spacious grounds, and a casual yet formal 7-course breakfast.

Each room offers a victorian theme, with the Queen Anne Room offering romantic accomodations, the highly sought Lightkeeper's room offering a view of the lighthouse from the bed, and the Mariners Room I offering accomodations said to be haunted. (Though we didn't find that to be the case when we stayed there!)

Enjoy a good night's sleep, wake up and enjoy your breakfast, learn all about the history of the home with a quick tour, and then stroll out to the lighthouse for a panoramic ocean view.

Note: You will be making reservations for 1 night. Plan on 1.5 hours for the breakfast.

Heceta Head Lighthouse Bed & Breakfast
92072 US-101
Yachats, OR 97498
541-547-3696
1-866-547-3696
www.HecetaLighthouse.com

Driving Directions: From the Cape Perpetua Lookout, return to Hwy 101. From here, travel south for 11.0 miles to Summer Street, the "guests only" road for parking at the Heceta Head Lighthouse Bed & Breakfast. Turn right / west here off of Hwy 101 and follow this to the parking for the B & B. Note: Summer Street IS NOT the paved road to the main Heceta Head Lighthouse parking area, which the public uses, but instead a small gravel road leading right off of Hwy 101 shortly after Mile Marker 178 and just before the paved road to the Heceta Head Lighthouse parking area. Summer Street tends to come up quickly on a rightward bend, so slow and be looking for it.

Note: If you are returning north onto Hwy 101 for whatever reason, be sure to read the important note about how to do so from Summer Street on Page 112.

Lodging Option: The Drift Inn & Cafe

Discover the Oregon Coast by day, stay in historic and unique hotels by night.

Tonight's choice of lodging falls partially under the category of historical, but perhaps more under the categories of unique, whimsical, and fun. Made up of a small campus consisting of 11 single rooms, small apartments, studio spaces and a 1930s Bungalow, The Drift Inn & Café provides travelers with inexpensive eclectic spaces offering views of the ocean, river, mountains and Yachats Bay. Better yet, with the café as part of the campus, an excellent meal awaits, be it breakfast, lunch or dinner.

Note: The Drift Inn & Café plays live music nightly.

> The Drift Inn Hotel & Cafe
> 124 US-101
> Yachats, OR 97498
> 541-547-4477
> www.The-Drift-Inn.com

Driving Directions: To reach the Drift Inn & Café, where you may have had breakfast this morning, you'll need to drive north on Hwy 101 back to Yachats. From the Heceta Head Lighthouse parking area, proceed east *under* Hwy 101 and turn right / north onto the highway. Proceed 11.1 miles to the Drift Inn & Café in Yachats, on your right.

Notes

Day Six

Heceta Head
To Coos Bay

Cape Arago Lighthouse

DAY 6
HECETA HEAD TO COOS BAY

Day 6 – Date: /   /

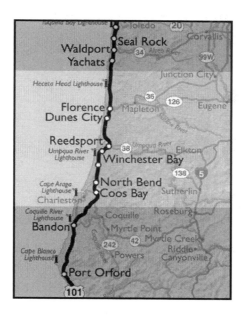

Summary: Where You're Going Today

- Heceta Head
- Florence, OR
- Dunes City, OR
- Coos Bay, OR

Today begins with a stroll through the quaint "old town" area of Florence, Oregon, where you'll explore small shops, cafes, galleries, a historical museum and more before continuing south to experience one of the wildest adventures on the Oregon Coast...riding the dunes on a high-speed sand rail. Next, you'll (hopefully) spot some majestic elk at the Dean Creek Elk Viewing Area before delving into the cultural, railroading and even printing history of the Coos Bay area.

Tonight's Lodging:

- Coos Bay Manor Bed & Breakfast

Today's Mileage: 61 Miles from Heceta Head to Coos Bay

Reservations Needed for This Segment:

- The Coos Bay Manor B & B - 541-290-9779 - 1 Night.

Start

Begin your day by driving south from Heceta Head to Florence, Oregon, where you'll stroll through the small old town area, and if it works with your schedule, enjoy some breakfast.

☐ **First Stop:** An Iconic View of Heceta Head

Begin your day by driving south on Hwy 101 for 0.8 mile to a large paved parking area on the right. From here, you'll look back north and enjoy seeing a beautiful view of the Heceta Head Lighthouse. It is because of this view that the Heceta Head Lighthouse is the most photographed lighthouse on the Oregon Coast.

 ☐ **Next Stop:** Florence, Oregon – Old Town District

Located just north of the 1936 Siuslaw River Bridge with art deco styling is the quaint beach town of Florence, Oregon. Be sure to spend some time here visiting the "Old Town" district, with its many different shops catering to tourists, including coffee shops, gift shops, bookstores, a bakery, an art gallery, a Mo's Seafood & Chowder house, various restaurants and more.

Driving Directions: From the viewpoint of Heceta Head, drive south on Hwy 101 for 11.7 miles into Florence, and turn left / south onto Maple Street. (You'll see a sign here directing you to Historic Old Town) Follow Maple Street for 3 blocks to Bay Street and the heart of the Old Town area.

☐ Next Stop: Edwin Kyle Bed & Breakfast

Just a few blocks west of the old town area is the Edwin K Bed & Breakfast. Walk on over to take a look at this restored 1914 Sears Craftsman home and stop in to get a sense of its charms so you'll know of another great place to stay for a future road trip or weekend visit to Florence and the Oregon Coast.

Edwin K Bed & Breakfast
1155 Bay Street
Florence, OR 97439
541-997-8360

Directions: From the corner of Maple Street and Bay Street, walk 3.5 blocks west to the Edwin K Bed & Breakfast.

☐ Next Stop: Siuslaw Pioneer Museum

Visit the Siuslaw Pioneer Museum to discover the natural and cultural history of the area, as well as learn about the lives of those who "lived, died, worked and played in the greater Siuslaw River Basin."

For those who would like a bit more immersive history, take the self-guided Historic Walking Tour, which leaves from the museum and visits 21 different buildings and locations in the Old Town Florence area.

Siuslaw Pioneer Museum
278 Maple Street
Florence, OR 97439
541-997-7884

- Open: Monday through Sunday – 12:00 p.m. to 4:00 p.m.

Directions: From the corner of Maple Street and Bay Street, walk north along Maple Street for 2 blocks to the museum.

☐ Next Stop: Sand Dunes Road

For an interesting, albeit short, Oregon Coast excursion, take a drive on Sand Dunes Road as it makes its way north through 6 miles of sand dunes to the mouth of the Siuslaw River.

Driving Directions: From Florence, return to Hwy 101 via Maple Street and proceed south for 1.1 miles to South Jetty Road / Sand Dunes Road. Turn right / west here and follow the road west and then north to the *South Jetty Dunes and Beach*.

 ## ☐ Next Stop: Guided Sand Rail Tours

It's time to put on your goggles, feel the breeze in your hair, and fill your shoes with sand!

Stretching 40 miles from Florence, OR down to Coos Bay, OR is the Oregon Dunes National Recreation Area, where the wind sculpts the ever-changing sand dunes into hills, bowls, plateaus, and ridges, sometimes reaching up to 500' high! And what better way to experience them than aboard a sand rail, a lightweight off-road and on-sand vehicle designed for high-speed thrills on the Oregon dunes.

We loved roaring across the sand, dropping over high lips, racing down steep faces, hitting exhilarating (though minor) jumps, and throwing rooster tails of sand the entire way. No doubt you will, too.

There are a few different tour providers on the coast, and here are two we'd recommend:

Sandland Adventures

Tours: ½ Hour Tour: $35 per person – 1 Hour Tour: $65 per person. Tours run rain or shine, so dress accordingly. Reservations are recommended, but not necessary. No refunds are given on tours within 72 hours of departure.

> Sandland Adventures
> 85366 Highway 101
> Florence, OR 97439
> 541-997-8087
> www.SandLand.com

Summer Hours:

> Monday through Friday – 9:00 a.m. to 5:00 p.m. with extended summer hours – Memorial Day weekend through September – Closed the first 4 days after Labor Day Monday.

Winter Hours:

> Tuesday through Saturday – 9:00 a.m. to 5:00 p.m. – October through December and March to Memorial Day Weekend.

Driving Directions: Return to Hwy 101 via South Jetty Road / Sand Dunes Road and turn right / south. You'll find Sandland Adventures immediately on your right.

Sand Dunes Frontier

Tours: ½ Hour Tour: $35 per person – 1 Hour tours during the off season: $65 per person. The last trip in the summer typically leaves sometime between 6:30 p.m. and 7:00 p.m. Trips go out rain or shine, and are first come, first served.

> Sand Dunes Frontier
> 83960 Hwy 101
> Florence, OR 97439
> 541-997-3544
> www.SandDunesFrontier.com

Summer Hours:

> Monday through Friday – 9:00 a.m. to 6:00 p.m.

Winter Hours:
> Tuesday through Saturday - December 15 to March 15 - 10:00 a.m. to 4:00 p.m.

Driving Directions: Return to Hwy 101 via South Jetty Road / Sand Dunes Road and turn right / south. Proceed for 2.9 miles to find Sand Dunes Frontier on your right.

☐ Next Stop: Umpqua Discovery Center

Experience the natural and cultural history of the Lower Umpqua Area through hands-on interpretive displays at the Umpqua Discovery Center. Here, you'll learn about the Kuuich Indians, the early pioneers, the important role logging played in this area, the natural history of the tidewater country, and much more.

Admission: Adults: $8.00 – Children (5-16): $4.00

Umpqua Discovery Center
409 Riverfront Way
Reedsport, OR 97467
541-271-4816

Summer Hours:

Monday through Saturday – 10:00 a.m. to 5:00 p.m. –
Sunday 12:00 p.m. to 4:00 p.m.

Winter Hours:

Monday through Saturday – 10:00 a.m. to 4:00 p.m. –
Sunday 12:00 p.m. to 4:00 p.m.

Driving Directions: From Sandland Adventures, continue south on Hwy 101 for 19.8 miles to the junction with Hwy 38 East / The Umpqua Highway. Turn left / east at the stop light and proceed 0.2 mile to East Railroad Avenue. Turn left / north here and follow this to Riverfront Way. Turn right here and proceed 1 block to find the museum on your left.

☐ Next Stop: Dean Creek Elk Viewing Area

Make a short 3.7 mile drive east of Reedsport, OR on Hwy 38 / the Umpqua River Scenic Byway to the Dean Creek Elk Viewing Area to see views of majestic Roosevelt Elk. While there is no guarantee the elk will be there at the time of your visit, the herd here can reach as many as 120 animals in size, and they are often seen early in the morning and at dusk.

Dean Creek Elk Viewing Area
48819 OR-38
Reedsport, OR 97467
541-756-0100

Driving Directions: From the Umpqua Discovery Center, drive east for 2 blocks on Riverfront Way to Hwy 38 East, which is now the Umpqua River Oregon Scenic Byway. From here, proceed east for 3 miles to the Dean Creek Elk Viewing Area.

☐ Next Stop: Umpqua River Light House & Museum

Initially built in 1857 near the mouth of the Umpqua River, and then rebuilt in 1894, the Umpqua River Lighthouse is a majestic though somewhat elusive piece of the Oregon Coast's history. Off limits behind a chain link fence, the 65' tall lighthouse with its distinctive red lens may only be accessed as part of a tour.

To arrange a tour of the lighthouse, visit the museum located one block to the north. Note that no tours are available after 4:00 p.m.

Umpqua River Lighthouse & Museum
1020 Lighthouse Road
Winchester Bay, OR 97467
541-271-4631

Open: Monday through Sunday – 10:00 a.m. to 4:00 p.m.

Driving Directions: Drive back on Hwy 38 to Hwy 101. From here, proceed south for 5.1 miles to Lighthouse Road, which leads to the Umpqua Lighthouse State Park. Turn right / west here and follow the signs for 0.8 mile to the lighthouse.

▢ Next Stop: Coos History Museum & Maritime Collection

The "anchor" of your visits while in Coos Bay is the impressive Coos History Museum & Maritime Collection. Showcasing the maritime, agricultural, and cultural history of the Coos Bay area and south Oregon coast, the museum's displays explore the  lives of the area's first inhabitants, as well as those of the early pioneers, and take a look at the logging, fishing and seafaring industries which helped to shape the region. In addition, visitors will find in the foyer an interesting display dedicated to noted Oregon middle and long-distance runner Steve Prefontaine, who lived in Coos Bay.

Coos History Museum
1210 North Front Street
Coos Bay, OR 97420
541-756-6320

- Open: Tuesday through Sunday – 10:00 a.m. to 5:00 p.m.

Driving Directions: Return to Hwy 101 from the Umpqua Lighthouse and drive south for 20.9 miles to North Front Street. Now, things get a little tricky here. From this turn, it appears that the Coos History Museum sits just off Hwy 101, but it actually sits off of North Front Street, which runs parallel to Hwy 101, and when turning left onto the poorly marked North Front Street, it appears you're turning into a parking lot, but turn left / north onto North Front Street and then follow this east to the museum.

Next Stop: Marshfield Sun Printing Museum

After visiting the Coos History Museum, walk over to the small Marshfield Sun Printing Museum building. Inside, you'll find the original antique printing presses, type cases, imposing tables, and other equipment, all arranged in its original layout, which was used in the printing of The Sun newspaper from 1891 to 1944. Admission is free, but donations are accepted.

Marshfield Sun Printing Museum
1049 North Front Street
Coos Bay, OR 97420
541-266-0901

- Open: Tuesday through Saturday – 1:00 p.m. to 4:00 p.m. – Memorial Day to Labor Day – Personal tours are available by appointment all year.

Walking Directions: Instead of driving, just walk southeast over to the printing museum from the Coos History Museum.

Next Stop: Oregon Coast Historical Railway

Situated behind a black iron fence next to Hwy 101 in Coos Bay is the growing collection of the Oregon Coast Historical Railway. A smartly painted 1922 Baldwin steam locomotive dominates the yard, and it's joined by a 1949 Alco S-2 diesel switcher engine, a 1942 steel caboose, a 1946-era wooden caboose, and an abundance of historical railroading and logging equipment.

Oregon Coast Historical Railway
800 South 1st Street
Coos Bay, OR 97420
541-267-6900

- Open: Wednesday *and* Saturday – 9:00 a.m. to 3:00 p.m.

Driving Directions: From the Coos History Museum, return to Hwy 101 and proceed south for 1.1 miles to Hall Ave. Turn left / east onto Hall, proceed 1 block, and then turn left / north. The Oregon Coast Historical Railway will be on your right.

www.Discover-Oregon.com

TONIGHT'S LODGING -
COOS BAY MANOR B & B

Step inside the historic 1912 Coos Bay Manor and feel the warmth of this grand Colonial Revival Style home welcome you for a memorable night's stay. Five individually themed rooms harken to a time of prestige on the Oregon Coast, though mixed with a few modern amenities. End your day with a good book in front of the fireplace, or perhaps relax and enjoy a slowly fading summer evening on the patio.

Mornings are greeted with coffee or tea served to your door, and you'll find a full breakfast conveniently served in the dining room anytime between 7:30 a.m. and 9:00 a.m. Those with dietary needs will find they are gladly accommodated.

- Check In: 4:00 p.m. to 6:00 p.m.
- Pets are not allowed.

Coos Bay Manor
955 S 5th Street
Coos Bay, OR 97420
541-290-9779
Reservations@CoosBayManor.com

Driving Directions: From the Oregon Coast Historical Railroad, drive north 1 block and turn left / west onto Golden Avenue. Cross Hwy 101 South while on Golden Avenue and proceed 3 blocks to S 5th Street. Turn left / south here and continue 2.5 blocks to the Coos Bay Manor.

Notes

DAY SEVEN

COOS BAY TO BANDON

Coquille River Lighthouse

DAY 7

COOS BAY TO BANDON

Day 7 – Date: /   /

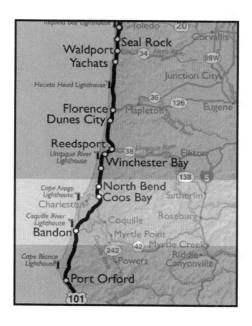

Summary: Where You're Going Today

- Charleston to Bandon Scenic Route
- Cape Arago Beach Loop
- Shore Acres State Park
- Bandon, OR

Heading south out of Charleston, Oregon today, you'll begin the Cape Arago Beach Loop, a delightful multi-stop drive which reveals some of the finest scenery on the south coast, and this is immediately followed with the Charleston to Bandon Scenic Byway, a tour route that leads you to the dramatic Coquille River Lighthouse and the welcoming

137

small town of Bandon, Oregon, with its collection of interesting shops, museums, an award-winning chocolatier, and the busy Tony's Crab Shack. Afterwards, you'll finish your day at the world-renowned Bandon Dunes Golf Resort, located on the edge of the Pacific Ocean.

Tonight's Lodging:

- The Bandon Dunes Golf Resort

Reservations Needed for This Segment:

- The Bandon Dunes Golf Resort – 800-742-0172 – Make reservations for 1 night

- Crabbing at Tony's Crab Shack in Bandon – No reservations are needed, but you'll want to set aside two or three hours in your day for this. If you don't have time to go crabbing, then simply order a fresh-caught and cooked crab to enjoy while dining outside.

Today's Mileage: 30 Miles from Charleston to Bandon

 Note: You may wish to top off your gas tank in Coos Bay this morning if you're getting low.

Start

There is plenty to see and do today, and you may want to sit for a while at some of the beautiful viewpoints along the way, so be sure not to tarry or dawdle this morning.

Charleston to Bandon
Scenic Tour Route

Pacific Ocean

North Bend

Coos Bay

Sunset Bay
State Park

Shore Acres
State Park

Charleston

Cape Arago
State Park

Seven Devils
State Rec. Park

Bandon Dunes
Golf Resort

Bullards Beach
State Park

Coquille River
Lighthouse

Bandon

Like the Three Capes Scenic Drive on Day 3, the Charleston to Bandon Scenic Tour Route is a meandering 41 mile byway along the scenic cliffs and beaches of the Oregon coastline, west of Hwy 101. Beginning with the Cape Arago Beach Loop, which leads travelers to a string of state parks, the scenic tour route then proceeds south along Seven Devils Road to Bandon, OR, where it then rejoins Hwy 101. Along the way it rewards travelers with panoramic ocean vistas, the beautiful landscaped gardens of Shore Acres State Park, a view of the Cape Arago Lighthouse, and the busy activities of over 1,000 seals and sea lions at Simpson Reef Overlook.

 ☐ **First Stop:** Cranberry Sweets & More

Located in both Coos Bay and old town Bandon, Cranberry Sweets & More showcases a bounty of cranberry products made from cranberries grown in the Bandon area, the *Cranberry Capital of Oregon*. Stop in at their Coos Bay factory store where you can watch candy being made during most weekdays, as well as "sample your heart out." Inside, you'll find jelly candies, toffees, brittles, fudge, cookies, caramels, assorted chocolates, salt water taffy, popcorn "& More".

Cranberry Sweets & More
1005 Newmark Ave.
Coos Bay, OR 97420
541-888-9824

- Open: Monday through Saturday – 9:30 a.m. to 5:30 p.m. – Sunday: 11:00 a.m. to 4:00 p.m.

Driving Directions: From the Coos Bay Manor, return to Hwy 101 *northbound*. From here, proceed north for 2.4 miles to Newmark Street. Turn left / west here, and follow this west for 2.5 miles to Cranberry Sweets & More on your left.

 Next Stop: University of Oregon Charleston Marine Life Center

Oregon State University has a number of satellite campuses across the state engaged in research, one of which is located right on the harbor in Charleston, OR. Open to the public, the Charleston Marine Life Center welcomes future marine biologists with a touch tank, salt water aquariums holding animals collected from the Oregon coast, (including Octopi) and five exhibit galleries focused on the animals, habitats and ecosystems of the coast.

Admission is $5, and children and students are free.

Charleston Marine Life Center
63466 Boat Basin Road
Charleston, OR 97420
541-888-2581

- Open: Wednesday through Saturday – 11:00 a.m. to 5:00 p.m.

Driving Directions: From Cranberry Sweets & More, continue west on Newmark Ave. for 0.4 mile to where it curves south and becomes the Cape Arago Highway. Continue south from this point for another 4.8 miles into Charleston, and turn right onto Boat Basin Road, shortly after crossing the bridge. You'll see the U of O Charleston Marine Life Center on your right in 1/2 mile.

☐ **Next Stop:** Cape Arago Beach Loop

 The Charleston to Bandon Scenic Tour Loop begins with a drive on the Cape Arago Beach Loop, which runs north to south as it passes a collection of beautiful state parks above the ocean waters. Along the way, you'll visit:

- Sunset Beach State Park
- Shore Acres State Park
- Simpson Reef Overlook
- Cape Arago Lookout

Upon reaching Cape Arago Lookout, you'll then retrace your route back to the Charleston to Bandon Scenic Tour Route.

 ☐ **Next Stop:** Sunset Bay State Park

Visit a scenic sandy beach tucked into a cove protected by rocky sea cliffs. The interpretive center here offers a number of services, including guided tidepool walks, nature walks, living history walks and Junior Ranger programs. Contact the Interpretive Center at 541-888-0982 for times and dates.

Open:

- May through June 15 – Friday through Sunday: 9:15 a.m. to 5:00 p.m.

- June 16 through September 15 – Open daily: 9:15 a.m. to 5:00 p.m.

Driving Directions: From the Charleston Marine Life Center, return to the Cape Arago Hwy and turn right / west. Follow this for 0.3 mile to where it turns into the Cape Arago Beach Loop. Continue to the 2.9 mile mark, where you'll find parking for Sunset Beach State Park.

 Next Stop: Shore Acres State Park

The weather and temperature on the Oregon Coast is perfect for growing plants during much of the year, so it's a bit of a wonder as to why there aren't more formal gardens dotting the coast. Shore Acres State Park certainly answers the call, as here travelers will find the beautifully landscaped grounds of a former lumber baron's estate. Walk the pathways, make your way through the boxwood lined flower gardens, wander to the quiet pond, visit the rose garden, and discover an abundance of plants blooming in a myriad colors, a few of which you may have never seen before in your life.

Afterwards, make your way to the large observation building or walk the path along the cliff top to see the rugged shoreline below, one of the most dramatic on the Oregon Coast, especially in rough weather. Don't forget to keep an eye out for whales.

Note: An Oregon State Parks Pass or fee is required here.

Driving Directions: From Sunset Beach State Park, proceed along the Cape Arago Beach Loop for 1.1 miles to the entrance for Shore Acres State Park.

  Next Stop: Simpson Reef Overlook

Simpson Reef Overlook is a fascinating and scenic "must stop". Here, the gradual slope of the offshore rocks and sandy beaches make this area the best location on the Oregon Coast for Stellar Sea Lions, California Sea Lions, Harbor Seals, and Northern Elephant Seals to "haul out", lay in the sun, and bark at each other. You'll likely hear over 1,000 of them out on the reef as soon as you get out of your car. Don't forget your binoculars.

Driving Directions: Continue on the Cape Arago Beach Loop for 1.0 mile to the Simpson Reef Overlook.

Next Stop: Cape Arago State Park

Continue 0.8 mile south to Cape Arago State Park to enjoy a stunning panoramic ocean view from a stone wall overlook on a bluff high above the ocean waves.

Next Stop: South Slough National Estuarine Research Center

An important part of Oregon's marine ecosystem, the salt flats, mud flats and channels of the South Slough provide a home for young Dungeness crab, oysters, shellfish, salmon and herring, as well as a varied collection of sea birds. Stop in at the South Slough National Estuarine Research Center to learn all about the South Slough through its impressive interpretive displays, as well as its collection of 10 short hikes ranging from .17 to .75 miles in length. In addition, be sure to say "Hello" to Ophelia, the Dungeness crab in the large saltwater tank in the entrance. A bit gregarious for a crab, don't be surprised if she comes to the front glass to greet you, which is nice, because we usually find Dungeness crabs to be a bit standoffish in social situations.

South Slough National Estuarine Research Center
61907 Seven Devils Road
Charleston, OR 97420
541-888-5558

- Open: Tuesday through Saturday – 10:00 a.m. to 4:30 p.m.

Driving Directions: From the Cape Arago Lookout, retrace your drive back north on the Cape Arago Beach Loop for 5.5 miles to Seven Devils Road. Turn right here and proceed south for another 4.2 miles to the entrance for the South Slough National Estuarine Research Center, on your left.

☐ **Next Stop:** Seven Devils Beach

If you're looking for a walk on a nice beach, then Seven Devils Beach is just the ticket. At 5.5 miles in length, it's a wide open expanse of shoreline just waiting to be explored. Note that the beach running north from the Coquille Lighthouse (your next stop) is a nice long beach, as well.

Driving Directions: From the South Slough National Estuarine Research Center, return to Seven Devils Road and turn left / south. Continue on Seven Devils Road for 6.5 miles (which becomes W Beaver Hill Road) to Whiskey Run Road / E Humphreys Road. Turn right / west here and continue on this for 2.5 miles as it connects again with Seven Devils Road. Turn right / north here and follow this for 1.6 miles to the left turn for Seven Devils Beach.

 ☐ **Next Stop:** Bullards Beach State Park & Coquille River Lighthouse

The drive from Hwy 101 through Bullards Beach State Park out to the Coquille River Lighthouse is a beautiful drive, which reminds us a little bit of portions of 17-Mile Drive along the Monterey Peninsula in California. Passing through the very nice and aptly

awarded "All Star" Bullards Beach State Park, the drive continues into the open along a spit of sand with the ocean just beyond the passenger side window. Soon, it finishes in a turnaround at the historic and picturesque 1896 Coquille Lighthouse, next to the Coquille River jetty.

Visitors are welcome to tour the lighthouse from 11:00 a.m. to 5:00 p.m., mid-May through September, when it is staffed with volunteers. The tower, however, is off limits due to safety concerns. For additional information, you may call the park office at 541-347-2209.

The 4.5 mile long beach stretching north from here is very nice for walking, and the jetty itself is also an interesting stroll, though it can be dangerous. Do not walk out on it if the seas are rough or the surface is wet! Also, do not

turn your back on the ocean. Note that there are a few picnic tables by the lighthouse, and this is a nice spot to enjoy a bite while watching fishing trawlers making their way out to sea and back.

For you photographers, you may find it handy to take photos of the lighthouse from the west. Position the small structure to the west of the base of the lighthouse within your frame such that it appears to be the base of the lighthouse tower.

Driving Directions: From Seven Devils Beach, return south on Seven Devils Road for 3.5 miles to Randolph Road. Turn left / east here and follow Randolph Road for 1.7 miles as it makes its way straight across Hwy 101 and meets up with N Bank Ln. Turn right here and follow this for 2.5 miles to Hwy 101. Turn right / *north* onto Hwy 101 and follow this for 0.1 mile before turning left / west onto Bullards Beach Road. Continue on this road for 3 miles as it makes its way through the State Park to the Coquille River Lighthouse. (We took you the scenic way!)

Bandon, Oregon

Your next handful of stops are in Bandon, Oregon. Home of the Bandon Cranberry Festival, this jewel of a coastal town offers visitors a lively historic district, a collection of interesting shops and galleries, a truly unique museum, world-class chocolates, and the perfect place to catch and eat your own Dungeness crab.

 ☐ **Next Stop:** Tony's Crab Shack

If it's time to eat, then Tony's Crab Shack is the place. Though its menu offers a wide selection of fresh seafood items, including ocean shrimp, wild prawns, local oysters, salmon, halibut, clams and much more, which are *"Always fresh – never fried."*, Tony's is known for its fresh Dungeness crab. Grab a table inside or out (you may have to wait a bit) and enjoy some fresh Oregon seafood while watching all the busy activity right on the water's edge.

Tony's Crab Shack
155 1st Street SE
Bandon, OR 97411
541-347-2875

- Open Monday through Sunday – 10:30 a.m. to 7:00 p.m. during the summer. Until 6:00 p.m. in winter.

 If you've never gone crabbing on the Oregon Coast, then now is the perfect time...and place...to give it a try, and whether you're a complete novice or seasoned pro, Tony's is more than happy to help out with all the equipment, advice, and tips you'll need to enjoy this iconic Oregon experience.

Attached to the restaurant is Tony's Port O' Call Tackle and Gifts, a one-stop shop for your  crabbing rentals. Here, you can buy a one-day crabbing license and rent a crab ring or trap, complete with a bucket and bait, for crabbing off the nearby docks, or if you're feeling a bit more adventurous you can also rent a small boat for crabbing in the bay. Once you've hauled in your catch, head the crew back to Tony's and they'll cook each crab for only $0.75 cents each, and for $3.00 each, they'll set you up with a plate, napkin, utensils, and a bit of melted butter to enjoy your meal.

 Before you begin, Tony's will give you plenty of advice, as well as a read on the current crabbing conditions. In a nutshell, crabbing is best one hour before to one hour after high tide, and if it hasn't rained lately, then all the better, as the bay will have less freshwater running through it. Be sure to allot at least two hours of time for your crabbing and ensuing meal.

Driving Directions: From the Coquille River Lighthouse, return to Hwy 101 and turn right / south. Proceed 2.9 miles to 2nd Street SE, as it veers off to the right, passing under the large sign spanning the road reading "Welcome to Old Town Bandon". In 2 blocks, turn right / north onto Baltimore Avenue SE and proceed one block to Tony's Crab Shack, to the left.

Next Stop: Washed Ashore Gallery

This is a "must see" attraction when you are in Bandon. Not only is its message important, but the large intricate works of art they create from ocean trash to educate a global audience about the extent of plastic pollution is downright amazing.

Washed Ashore Gallery & Workshop
325 2nd Street SE
Bandon, OR 97411
541-329-0317

Summer Hours:

- Mid-June through mid-September – Tuesday through Saturday 11:00 a.m. to 5:00 p.m.

Winter Hours:

- Mid-September through mid-June – Thursday through Saturday – 12:00 p.m. to 5:00 p.m.

Walking Directions: From Tony's, walk east on 1st Street SE for 1.5 blocks and turn right onto Chicago Ave SE. Walk 1 block south and find the Washed Ashore Gallery at 325 2nd Street SE.

Next Stop: Coastal Mist Chocolates

Every Oregon Road Trip involves fine chocolates, and on this trip you can find them at Coastal Mist Chocolates in Old Town Bandon. Savor their world-class artisan chocolates, European style desserts and pastries, gourmet sandwiches, decadent truffles and more.

Coastal Mist Chocolates
210 2nd Street SE
Bandon, OR 97411
541-347-3300

- Open: Monday through Thursday – 11:00 a.m. to 5:30 p.m., Friday and Saturday – 10:00 a.m. to 6:00 p.m., and Sunday – 10:00 a.m. to 5:00 p.m.

Walking Directions: Walk 1 block west on 2nd Street SE.

Next Stop: Bandon Historical Society Museum

Housed in the former Bandon City Hall, the second building built after the great fire of 1936, the Bandon Historical Society Museum contains a wealth of items which showcase the city's history, tragic shipwrecks, industries that shaped Bandon's past, and the cultural and natural history of the region.

Bandon Historical Society Museum
270 Fillmore Ave. SE
Bandon, OR 97411
541-347-2164

- Open: Monday through Friday – 10:00 a.m. to 4:00 p.m.

Driving Directions: From Coastal Mist Chocolates proceed 2 blocks east on 2nd Street SE to Hwy 101, and then continue another 2 blocks east on Hwy 101 to the Bandon Historical Museum on the southwest corner of Filmore Ave. and Hwy 101.

 Next Stop: Face Rock Creamery

 Stop in at the Face Rock Creamery to see how their award-winning cheeses are made, as well as sample an abundance of different cheeses, some hand-scooped ice cream, tasty chocolates, and more.

Face Rock Creamery
680 2nd Street SE
Bandon, OR 97411
541-347-3223

- Open: Monday through Sunday – 9:00 a.m. to 6:00 p.m.

Walking Directions: From the Bandon Historical Museum, walk east on Hwy 101 for 1 long block to the Face Rock Creamery.

☐ Next Stop: Coquille Point & The Bandon Sea Stacks

Stop at Coquille Point on your way to Face Rock and enjoy a beautiful 180 degree view of Bandon's many sea stacks, including Table Rock, Five Foot Rock, Sisters, Wash Rock and Face Rock, which is only ½ mile to the south. In addition, make your way down the long staircase to the beach below during low tide and walk amongst the sea stacks or take a walk on the flat paved interpretive trail found at the top of the stairs.

Driving Directions: From the Face Rock Creamery, drive west on Hwy 101 for 0.6 miles as it curves south, and then turn right / west onto 11th Street SW. Follow this west through the City Park for 1 mile to the parking area and viewpoint.

☐ Next Stop: Face Rock Viewpoint

Like some surreal sculpture, Bandon's Face Rock looks just like a human face forever locked in a skyward gaze. It's uncanny how geologic chance captured this "look", which becomes even more apparent with the shadows of later in the day.

Driving Directions: From the viewpoint, return east 1 block to Beach Loop Road and turn right. Proceed 0.6 mile to Face Rock.

Tonight's Lodging - Bandon Dunes Golf Resort

Your busy day ends at the world-renowned Bandon Dunes Golf Resort, where you'll definitely enjoy your stay, whether you're a golfer or not.

Perched high above the Pacific Ocean and surrounded by beautiful greens and towering dunes, Bandon Dunes Golf Resort welcomes travelers with a mix of single and double occupancy rooms, suites and cottages, offering king and queen beds, private baths, TV, Wi-Fi and other amenities, as well as views of the ocean and different courses or the dunes and surrounding woods.

Guests can enjoy walking along the resort's 10 miles of pathways offering views of the five different golf courses and the ocean, or enjoy the sauna, whirl pool, massage center or fitness center. Afterwards, enjoy dining and drinks at one of the six restaurants or pubs on site, which offer the finest in Northwest cuisine, fine wines, local microbrews and, of course, classic single malt scotches.

- Check In: 4:00 p.m.
- Check Out: 11:00 a.m.
- It is suggested guests book at their earliest convenience, as the resort is busy year round.
- Pets are not allowed due to wildlife in the area.

Bandon Dunes Golf Resort
57744 Round Lake Road
Bandon, OR 97411
541-347-4380
800-742-0172

Note: Be sure to hike up to the top of the small bluff immediately east of the lodge to enjoy the nice view of Bandon Dunes before leaving.

Driving Directions: From Face Rock, return to Hwy 101 via 11th Street SW. Here, turn left / *north* and follow this 6.1 miles to Randolph Road. Turn left / west here and follow this for 1.5 miles to Round Lake Road. Turn right / north here and follow the signs to Bandon Dunes Golf Resort.

Lodging Option: The Coos Bay Manor B & B

If you'd rather not stay at the Bandon Dunes Golf Resort, you may wish to stay where you stayed last night, at the Coos Bay Manor B & B, 20 miles north. (See Page 134)

DAY EIGHT

BANDON TO GOLD BEACH

Cape Blanco Lighthouse

DAY 8
BANDON TO GOLD BEACH

Day 8 – Date: /   /

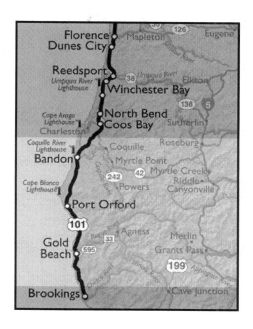

Summary: Where You're Going Today

- Bandon, OR
- Cape Blanco State Park & Lighthouse
- Port Orford, OR
- Gold Beach
- Samuel H. Boardman Scenic Corridor
- Gold Beach (Again)

Today, you'll travel south to Gold Beach, which is where you'll be staying tonight. However, you'll continue south past Gold Beach today to visit 10 different scenic sites within the Samuel H. Boardman Scenic Corridor, reaching your farthest point south on this road trip before returning back north to Gold Beach for the evening.

Tonight's Lodging:

- The Rogue River Lodge at Snag Patch

Today's Mileage: 100 Miles

Reservations Needed for This Segment:

- Rogue River Lodge at Snag Patch - 541-247-0101
  - Make a reservation for *at least* 1 night
  - Important: See Page 186 for additional instructions on why you may make another night's reservation here or elsewhere.

Before You Leave:

Fill your gas tank in Bandon this morning.

Start

Leave the Bandon Dunes Golf Resort and make your way south through Bandon on Hwy 101.

First Stop: West Coast Game Park Safari

Located just south of Bandon on US-101 is the West Coast Game Park Safari, a walk-through safari park where visitors can view, interact with, and photograph over 450 animals, including African Lions, Bengal Tigers, Snow Leopards, cougars, bears, zebras, bison, camels, chimpanzees, deer and many others. Springtime is especially fun, as it provides once-in-a-lifetime opportunities to interact with young lions, tigers, leopards and other wild animals. Plan on taking about one hour here.

Rates range from $11.00 to $21.00. Children under 2 are free.

West Coast Game Park Safari
46914 US-101
Bandon, OR 97411
541-347-3106

- Open: Monday through Sunday – 10:00 a.m. to 5:00 p.m. Note: Last entry is at 4:30 p.m.

Driving Directions: From the Bandon Dunes Golf Resort, return to Highway 101 and proceed south for 13.3 miles, where you'll find the West Coast Game Park Safari on your right.

☐ **Next Stop:** New River Nature Center

Take a moment to discover the New River Nature Center. Located up a short road off of Hwy 101, this small but impressive nature center explains the habitats and ecosystems of the nearby New River Area of Critical Environmental Concern, an area offering miles of trails,  waterways, and beaches for exploring.

New River Nature Center
86434-86442 Croft Lake Road
Bandon, OR 97411

- Open: Tuesday – Sunday – 10:00 a.m. to 4:00 p.m.

Driving Directions: From the West Coast Game Park Safari, continue south on Hwy 101 for 1.4 miles to Croft Lake Road. Turn right / west here and proceed 2.0 miles to the New River Nature Center.

☐ **Next Stop:** Dragonfly Farm & Nursery

Part of the Wild Rivers Coast Farm Trail, which runs from Bandon, OR to Port Orford, OR and supplies local vendors with local farm produce for visitors to enjoy, Dragonfly Farm offers a large variety of unique and indigenous plants, all in a setting surrounded by  tall coastal firs. Stop in to see what's growing on the Oregon Coast, and keep an eye out for the free-roaming chickens!

Dragonfly Farms & Nursery
49295 Highway 101
Langlois, OR 97450
541-844-5559

- Open: Wednesday through Saturday – 10:00 a.m. to 4:00 p.m., Sunday – 11:00 a.m. to 4:00 p.m.

Driving Directions: From the New River Nature Center, return to Hwy 101 and from here proceed south for 2.9 miles to the entrance to the nursery, on your left. Note that it is the first driveway on the left after passing the "Entering Curry County" sign, just before Mile Marker 286."

Next Stop: Cape Blanco State Park and Cape Blanco Lighthouse

First lit in December of 1870, the historic Cape Blanco Lighthouse is not only Oregon's southernmost lighthouse, but it also occupies the farthest point west in the state. Visit the nearby gift shop to purchase a ticket for the tour, and learn all about  the lighthouse and the keepers who lived on the cape.

Tickets for lighthouse tours are $2 for adults 16 and older. 15 and under are free of charge.

Cape Blanco Lighthouse
91100 Cape Blanco Road
Port Orford, OR 97465
541-332-2207

- Open: Wednesday through Monday (Closed Tuesdays) – April through October 31st - 10:00 a.m. to 3:15 p.m. The last tour ticket is sold at 3:15, but this doesn't give you enough time to tour the lighthouse and hear about its history. Gates close at 3:30 p.m.

Driving Directions: From Dragonfly Farm & Nursery, proceed south on Hwy 101 for 10.5 miles to Cape Blanco Road. Turn right / west here and follow this for 5.3 miles along a nice drive to the Cape Blanco Lighthouse.

☐ Next Stop: Patrick Hughes House

 Located within Cape Blanco State Park and just off the drive to the Cape Blanco Lighthouse, is the beautiful 1898 Queen Anne style home of Patrick and Jane Hughes. Restored and well curated with impressive period-specific furnishings, the home and its volunteers welcome visitors to learn about the Hughes, their lives in the area, and their seven children, one of which was a keeper at the nearby Cape Blanco Lighthouse. Tours are free, but donations are gladly accepted to help fund the continued restoration and maintenance of the home.

Patrick Hughes House
91816 Cape Blanco Road
Port Orford, OR 97465
541-332-0248

- Open: Wednesday through Monday (Closed Tuesdays) – April through October 31st - 10:00 a.m. to 3:30 p.m.

Driving Directions: From the Cape Blanco Lighthouse, drive back on Cape Blanco Road towards Hwy 101 for 1.4 miles before turning left / north towards the Patrick Hughes House.

☐ Next Stop: Port Orford Lifeboat Station Museum

Beginning in 1934 and continuing into the 1960s, the Port Orford Lifeboat Station housed Surfmen, who would answer the call of ships in distress by racing down 532 steps to Nellie's Cove and courageously row a rescue boat out into rough seas to save the lives of imperiled sailors. Today, you can visit and tour the museum housed in the former barracks to learn about

 the role of the Lifeboat Station and the men stationed here. In addition, you can walk the grounds, see a restored 36 foot self-righting lifeboat, and take a hike down to Nellie's Cove. Note: If you'd like a fun souvenir, have a custom dog tag made while at the museum.

The museum and tour are free, though donations are gladly accepted.

Port Orford Lifeboat Station
92331 Coast Guard Hill Road
Port Orford, OR 97465
541-332-0521

- Open: Wednesday through Monday (Closed Tuesdays) – April through October 31st - 10:00 a.m. to 3:30 p.m.

Driving Directions: From the Patrick Hughes House, return to Hwy 101 and continue south from here for 4.3 miles to Port Orford, turning right / west onto 9th Street. Follow 9th Street west for 2 blocks and then turn left onto the Port Orford "Highway". Follow this for 0.8 mile to the Lifeboat Station.

Note: You'll soon be passing through Gold Beach, Oregon, which is where you'll be staying this evening. However, continue south now to 10 different stops along the Samuel H. Boardman State Scenic Corridor before returning back north to Gold Beach later today.

☐ Next Stop: The Isaac Lee Patterson Memorial Bridge

If you appreciate fine engineering and architecture mixed with Oregon history, then you'll enjoy this next stop.

Prior to the 1930s, travelers along the Oregon coast would have to cross major rivers and bays by ferryboat, which added considerable time to their trip as they waited for the ferry to return, then to board, and then to cross. If the weather was poor, the rivers flooded, or the ferryboat wasn't working, then they were at the mercy of time. Beginning in the early 1930s, highway engineer Conde McCullough designed and built a series of bridges along the length of the Oregon coast which eliminated this problem and eased travel burdens considerably. With seven impressive spans showcasing the Art Deco style of the period, the 1931 Isaac Lee Patterson Memorial bridge is one of the finest examples of Mr. McCullough's work.

Perhaps the best place to see the bridge during the morning hours, when the light comes from the east, is at Lex's Landing, just to the east of its northern end.

If you'd like to learn more about the engineering and construction of Oregon's coastal bridges, we highly recommend the book *Lifting Oregon Out of the Mud - Building the Oregon Coast Highway*, by Joe R. Blakely. Look for it at gift shops and bookstores along the coast.

> **Lifting Oregon Out of the Mud**
> Building the Oregon Coast Highway
>
> by Joe R. Blakely

Driving Directions: From the Port Orford Lifeboat Station, return to Hwy 101 and travel south for 26.5 miles to the northern end of the bridge.

☐ **Next Stop:** Kissing Rock

Only minutes south of Gold Beach, Kissing Rock, being next to Hwy 101, offers easy beach access and is a great place to watch surfers catching some waves.

Driving Directions: Kissing Rock is approximately 2 miles south of Gold Beach.

☐ **Next Stop:** Cape Sebastian Viewpoint & Trail

Turn right off of Hwy 101 and take the short road through a Sitka Spruce forest to the south parking lot. Take the 1.5 mile trail here out to the cape to enjoy a stunning panoramic view, and then continue down to the beach at Hunter's Cove.

Driving Directions: From Kissing Rock, drive south for 4.2 miles to the right / west turn for Cape Sebastian Viewpoint.

Next Stop: Samuel H. Boardman State Scenic Corridor

Stretching for 12 linear miles along the southern Oregon Coast, just north of the California border, is the Samuel H. Boardman State Scenic Corridor. Honoring its namesake, whom is widely recognized as the father of the Oregon State Parks system, this collection of 11 scenic viewpoints and points of interest encapsulates some of the most scenic and dramatic coastline of the entire Oregon coast and features stunning vistas, rugged shorelines, sandy beaches, and more. In addition, most points make excellent locations from which to spot whales as they journey north and south.

There are actually two different Samuel H. Boardman State Scenic Corridors; one that visitors see from the pullout or parking lot at each destination, and the other which they experience after taking the brief hike found at most locations. We strongly encourage you to hike beyond the parking areas and down the different trails so as to enjoy a much more dramatic and awe-inspiring coastline. Note: In the descriptions that follow, you'll see two numbers reflecting our rating for that site. The first rates the site based upon what you'll see from the parking area, and the second rates the same site, but after hiking the trail to a nearby viewpoint, meadow, or beach. As you'll see in all cases, it's much more rewarding to leave the parking lot and explore the (usually) short trails.

☐**Next Stop:** Arch Rock – 6 / **10** - (Mile 344.8)

Offering one of the best ocean views in the Scenic Corridor, Arch Rock Point is reached via a short paved path that leads to beautiful views of sea stacks and Arch Rock itself.

Driving Directions: From Cape Sebastian, drive south on Hwy 101 for 9.9 miles to the right turn for Arch Rock.

☐**Next Stop:** Spruce Island & Secret Beach – 2/8 (Mile 345.0)

Spruce Island, Secret Beach, and Thunder Rock Cove all have roadside pullouts, beginning with Spruce Island on the north end, at Mile 345.0. Park here and take the trail south through a Sitka Spruce forest to a close up look at a collection of large sea stacks, and then either continue south on the trail to Secret Beach, which is very scenic, or return to your car and proceed to the parking area for Secret Beach at Mile 345.3. Keep an eye out for some unofficial yet very handy hand-drawn maps near the trailheads.

Driving Directions: Drive south on Hwy 101 from Arch Rock for 0.2 miles to a somewhat large parking area on your right.

☐ Next Stop: Thunder Rock Cove – 0 / **10** - (Mile 345.8)

Just south of Secret Beach is the Thunder Rock Cove Viewpoint. Take the short dirt trail, which begins on the northern end of the parking lot, to the cove. Here, you'll find outstanding views of the rugged coastline and dramatic rock formations below.

Driving Directions: From the Spruce Island parking area, drive south on Hwy 101 for 0.8 mile. (1.0 mile from Arch Rock)

☐ Next Stop: Natural Bridges – 0 / **7** - (Mile 346.0)

A short paved trail and wooden walkway quickly takes you to one of the more well-known features of the Scenic Corridor, the Natural Bridges.

Directions: From Thunder Rock Cove, drive south for 0.2 mile to Natural Bridges.

☐ Next Stop: North Island – 0 / **6** - (Mile 347.4)

Find the trail on the south end of the parking area and make your way through the forest before breaking out into an overgrown "meadow", which leads down into a bowl, terminating at a ledge high above the surf. Note that if it has rained recently, your pants will get wet as you hike through all of the overgrowth.

Driving Directions: From Natural Bridges, proceed south for another 1.4 miles to North Island.

☐ Next Stop: Indian Sands – 3 / **6** - (Mile 348.6)

With Indian Sands, you'll hike ½ mile down to a collection of sandstone features high above the waterline. Note that the sand here isn't from the ocean, but instead from an exposed sandstone bluff above the high tide line.

Driving Directions: Continue south on Hwy 101 for 1.2 miles.

☐ Next Stop: Whaleshead Beach – 2 / **8** - (Mile 349.3)

Just before reaching the Whaleshead Beach RV Resort, turn right and make your way down a short and sometimes rough road to a large paved parking area with restrooms, and then follow the short trail from here to Whaleshead Beach, a long and beautiful beach with sea stacks. Note, this road is sometimes impassable in large mobile homes, and it may take a little finesse to get your car down to the parking area. There is a sign recommending 4 wheel drive vehicles, but there was a Prius in the parking lot when we last arrived.

Driving Directions: Continue driving south for 0.7 mile to Whaleshead Beach.

☐ Next Stop: House Rock – 3 / **10** - (Mile 351.2)

Simply drive to the parking area and climb 7 wide steps to a short paved path that leads to a 180+ degree panoramic view, dedicated to Samuel H. Boardman.

Driving Directions: Proceed south on Hwy 101 for another 1.9 miles to House Rock.

☐ Next Stop: Cape Ferrelo – **8** - (Mile 351.9)

Cape Ferrelo is a small viewpoint with a nice view, and look for wildflowers here in the spring. Note that the parking area is small, so there is no trailer turnaround available.

Driving Directions: From House Rock, travel south on Hwy 101 for 0.7 mile to the turnoff for Cape Ferrelo Viewpoint.

Next Stop: Lone Ranch Picnic Area – **10** - (Mile 352.6)

This is a large open park with 10 picnic tables lining a short path to a long beach punctuated with sea stacks and piles of driftwood. You'll find easy access in and out of the large paved parking area.

Driving Directions: Continue south for another 0.7 mile to the Lone Ranch Picnic Area, your last stop in the Samuel H. Boardman State Scenic Corridor.

Note: You'll now drive back north for 25 miles to Gold Beach, Oregon, where you'll stay the night.

Tonight's Lodging - Rogue River Lodge Gold Beach, OR

Imagine a cozy and comfortable yet upscale historic motor lodge with well appointed rooms, private backyards with hot tubs on a deck surrounded by beautiful landscaping, and views of the Rogue River and you have the Rogue River Lodge at Snag Patch. Choose from 8 different rooms and suites, all with luxurious amenities, and be sure to take the time to enjoy your view of the river, especially in the morning when it is active with birds, fish and seals.

A "Yummy Lite Breakfast" is served each morning, and if you're lucky, you may get to enjoy some of Michael's amazing smoked salmon as part of your meal.

Note: See Page 186 before making your reservations for this evening.

Rogue River Lodge at Snag Patch
94966 N Bank Rogue River Road
Gold Beach, OR 97444
541-247-0101

- Check-In: 3:00 p.m.
- Check-Out: 11:00 a.m.
- 48 Hour cancellation policy.
- No smoking is allowed within the rooms.
- No pets are allowed.
- Complimentary Wi-Fi is available.
- Unfortunately, children under 10 are not allowed during the summer months.
- Each room comes with a complimentary light breakfast in the main area, consisting of waffles, fruit, yogurt, coffee, tea and juice.

Driving Directions: Return to Gold Beach. From the northern end of the Isaac Lee Patterson Memorial Bridge over the Rogue River, turn right / east onto N Bank Rogue River Road and follow this for just under 3 miles to the Rogue River Lodge at Snag Patch. Look for the driveway to the lodge as it veers off to the right and drops down from the road.

Note: If you look up the Rogue River Lodge online, be aware that there are two other Rogue River Lodges; The Rogue River Lodge in Trail, Oregon and Morrison's Rogue River Lodge in Merlin, Oregon. The Rogue River Lodge you want is the one at Snag Patch, just east of Gold Beach, Oregon.

Lodging Option #1: Tu Tu' Tun Lodge

Located on the north bank a few miles upriver from the Rogue River Lodge is the luxurious Tu Tu' Tun Lodge. Surrounded by expansive well-manicured grounds, the lodge welcomes guests

with a sense of serenity as the smooth waters of the Rogue flow past. Explore the area, sit by the river with a glass of wine, savor the fine cuisine of a five-course dinner, and then retire to the comfort of your well appointed room, suite or house, all with a view of the river.

> Tu Tu' Tun Lodge
> 96550 N Bank Rogue River Rd.
> Gold Beach, OR 97444
> 541-247-6664

Driving Directions: Return to Gold Beach. From the northern end of the Isaac Lee Patterson Memorial Bridge over the Rogue River, turn right / east onto N Bank Rogue River Road and follow this for 3.7 miles to where N Bank Rogue River Road makes a 90 degree right turn. Continue to follow this road until you reach the driveway for the Tu Tu' Tun Lodge at the 6.7 mile mark from the Isaac Lee Patterson Memorial Bridge. It is a right hand turn into the driveway.

Lodging Option #2: Pacific Reef Resort

 Offering travelers their choice of a hotel, motel, beachfront condos or vacation rentals, all close to the ocean, the Pacific Reef Resort is an excellent place to stay while in Gold Beach. Ocean view rooms with private decks are perfect for watching the sunset, and afterwards, you can watch a family movie on the big screen set up outside.

Pacific Reef Resort
29362 Ellensburg Hwy 101
Gold Beach, OR 97444
541-247-6658

Driving Directions: You'll find the Pacific Reef Resort immediately west of Hwy 101 in Gold Beach.

Notes

DAY NINE

JET BOATING ON THE WILD AND SCENIC ROGUE RIVER

Umpqua River Lighthouse

DAY 9
JET BOATING ON THE WILD
AND SCENIC ROGUE RIVER

Day 9 – Date: /   /

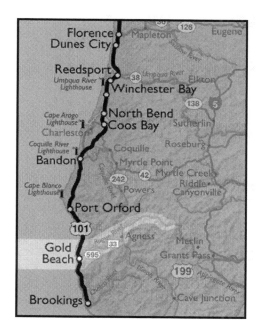

Summary: Where You're Going Today

- Jerry's Rogue Jets on the Rogue River

Today, your Oregon Coast road trip ends on a high note! You'll board a high speed jet boat in Gold Beach and make your way 52, 64 or 104 miles roundtrip on the scenic Rogue River, with each trip showcasing the beauty, flora and fauna of this exciting Oregon adventure. It's a true taste of Oregon summer fun!

Tonight's Lodging:

- If you're not starting home right after the Jet Boat tour, then book a second night at either the Rogue River Lodge in Gold Beach, a hotel you stayed in previously during this road trip, or head over to the Willamette Valley and stay a night at the historic Weasku Inn or Wolf Creek Inn. See Page 186 for additional details.

Today's Mileage: 64, 80, or 104 Miles

Reservations Needed for This Segment:

- The Weasku Inn: 541-471-8000
  or
- The Wolf Creek Inn: Reserve America at 800-452-5687
  or
- A Hotel of Your Choice

- Jerry's Rogue River Jet Boats – 800-451-3645
  - Make reservations for one of the following:
    - 64 Mile Historic Mail Route
    - 80 Mile Whitewater Excursion
    - 104 Mile Wilderness Whitewater

Before You Leave:

 You may want to fill your gas tank in Gold Beach before heading home.

Start

Simply drive from your lodging to Jerry's Rogue River Jet Boats, located on the south side of the Isaac Lee Patterson Memorial Bridge / Rogue River Bridge.

☐ **Today's Stop**: A Rogue River Jet Boat Excursion

Imagine flying atop a scenic Oregon river at over 40 mph with 100' high rock walls whipping by so close to the boat that you're sure you could reach out and touch them. Breaking out into an open stretch of water, your guide hits the gas as the boat begins to dive left, suddenly careening into a 180 degree spin, followed by a huge splash of water...and everybody aboard bursting into laughter and applause.

Oregon Coast adventure awaits on a jet boat ride up the scenic Rogue River from Gold Beach, OR. Choose from a menu of three family-friendly trips, all with a knowledgeable and skilled river guide who will provide a narrated overview of the river, its plentiful flora and  fauna, the impressive geologic features you'll pass through, and stories about famous movies shot on the river itself, all with a boatload of thrills and laughs along the way. Keep your eyes out for bears and deer on the bank, Bald Eagles flying overhead, Great Blue Herons nesting in the fir trees, and a salmon or two tugging at the lines of fishermen as you pass by.

Season: May 1st through mid-October

Tours:

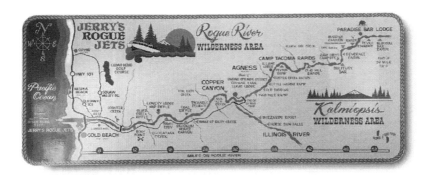

- **64 Mile Historic Mail Route**

  A casual and scenic 64 mile round-trip jet boat excursion without any whitewater. Plan on 4.5 hours, which includes a 1 hour meal stop at Agness, OR, on the river. The jet boat fare does not include the cost of your meal.

  Departure Times:

  - May 15 to June 30 - 9:30 a.m.
  - July 1 to August 31 – 9:30 a.m. & 3:00 p.m.
  - September 1 to Oct. 15 – 9:30 a.m.

  Fares:

  - Adult: $50
  - Child (4 to 11): $25.00
  - 3 And under: Free

- **80 Mile Whitewater Excursion**

  Perfect for those who want a bit of whitewater adventure. You'll pass over and through 6 different sets of rapids along your 80 mile round-trip excursion. Plan on stopping periodically along the way for photo opportunities, to watch a fisherman battle a salmon, view and learn about the wildlife, and more. This trip takes 4.75 hours, and stops for a 1 hour meal break, which is not included in the price of your trip.

  Departure Times:

  - June 15 to June 30 – 12:00 p.m.
  - July 1 to August 31 – 8:45 a.m., 12:00 p.m. & 2:15 p.m.
  - September 1 to September 15 – 12:00 p.m.

  Fares:

  - Adult: $70
  - Child (4 to 11): $35.00
  - 3 And under: Free

- **104 Mile Wilderness Whitewater**

  It's a full day of whitewater adventure on the majestic Rogue River! The 104 mile round-trip takes boaters into the 'Wild" section of the river, which can be reached only by rafting, hiking, and jet boating. You'll learn about the history of the river along the way from your skilled guide, as well as race through the canyons while keeping an eye out for bears, river otters, osprey, bald eagles and more.

  Departure Times:

  - May 1 to June 30 – 9:00 a.m.
  - July 1 to August 31 – 8:15 a.m. & 11:30 a.m.
  - September 1 to September 30 – 9:00 a.m.

Fares:

- Adult: $95
- Child (4 to 11): $45.00
- 3 And under: Free

Plan to arrive and check in at least 15 to 30 minutes prior to your departure time.

What to Wear:

You'll want to dress in layers, especially during the spring season of May through early June, when the weather is less stable and the water is cooler, as well as the month of September, when the water is warmer, but the air is cooler in the afternoons. With the coastal fog, you will find you're pretty well bundled up when you depart Gold Beach, but once you're up river 15 miles or so, you may find yourself in the warm sunshine. Keep in mind, however, that while you may spend the afternoon in a t-shirt, you'll want as much warmth as you can muster during the last 10 miles downriver as you speed back into the coastal fog. Bring a hat, windbreaker, warm coat and wind pants *if it will be foggy upon your return to Gold Beach.* (Do not underestimate this!) Call Jerry's on the day of your trip to get a sense of the weather. Note that we've been splashed on the jet boats, but not soaked. That doesn't mean you won't be, however.

During the summer months, you can expect highs in the 80s and 90s, so typical summer attire is fine. *Be sure to bring sunscreen, sunglasses and water.* A hat is also advised, since you'll be in the sun for much of the time during the longer trips upriver.

 FYI, we found it beneficial to bring a small pair of binoculars for viewing wildlife. We were fortunate to spot bear cubs on the two trips we've taken.

Jerry's Rogue Jets
29985 Harbor Way
Gold Beach, OR 97444
800-451-3645

Note: For those wanting to add another day to their trip, as well as a bit more exploration, you have the option of staying overnight at Paradise Lodge 52 miles upriver. Bring an overnight bag with a change of clothes and sundries, and enjoy the ride upriver to the lodge, where you'll stay the night before catching the return boat back to Gold Beach the next day. We enjoyed the overnight stay, but we're hesitant to recommend it to others until Paradise Lodge fixes a problem they have with their cabins, and that is that their gas fireplaces vent exhaust out the front of the fireplace *directly into your room*, which makes your room smell a bit foul the entire time you're there, even if it is just the pilot light that is burning. Inquire with Jerry's Rogue Jets if you'd like to add this option to your 104 mile trip, and don't forget to add the additional day to your dates in this book.

Driving Directions: You'll find Jerry's Rogue Jets to the northwest of Hwy 101, 0.3 mile south of the southern end of the Isaac Lee Patterson Memorial Bridge over the Rogue River.

Your Road Trip is finished! - 3 Choices for Heading Home

Your Oregon Coast Road Trip is now finished! Having wrapped up on the beautiful southern Oregon Coast, you may find yourself a ways from home. If you can't simply drive home to finish your last day, *then you may want to book an additional night in a historic hotel, inn or bed & breakfast during your journey back home.* We recommend the following choices:

- If you're driving back north and prefer to take Hwy 101, you may choose to stay another night in one of the hotels you enjoyed during your road trip. *If that's the case, then be sure to book tonight's stay when making your initial reservations.* For example, if you want to stay tonight in The Channel House in Depoe Bay, then when booking your first night for Day 3 of this trip, you'd also book a night for tonight, Day 9.

- If you're driving back north or south and prefer to drive on I-5, then you may wish to "cross over" east to the Grants Pass area before beginning your drive and stay at the historic **Weasku Inn** or the charming **Wolf Creek Inn**, just up I-5 a ways in Wolf Creek, OR. Note: If you plan on taking the Bear Camp Coastal Route/Galice Creek Road/NF 23 over the Coast Range, between Gold Beach and Galice/Grants Pass, *be aware that travel on this road is not advised and can be dangerous between November 5th and May 31st, especially if there is snow on the ground.*

The Wolf Creek Inn and Tavern

Built in 1883, the historic Wolf Creek Inn holds the distinction of being the oldest continuously operating inn in the Pacific Northwest. Its eight period-specific rooms welcome travelers for only $80 per night. Note that the inn does not serve meals, but the family friendly Ricki's Place restaurant is next door. Reservations for the inn may be made via Reserve America at 800-452-5687.

Wolf Creek Inn State Heritage Site
100 Front Street
Wolf Creek, OR 97497
800-452-5687
541-866-2474
wolfcreek.inn@oregon.gov

The Weasku Inn

 It's hard to decide what is best about the Weasku Inn. Is it the friendly staff? The warm chocolate chip cookies awaiting guests in the evening? Perhaps it's the well-appointed rooms with comfortable beds? Or maybe it's that welcome feeling you get when you open the large wooden door and walk into the cozy lobby while nostalgic music softly plays.

You'll definitely enjoy your stay at the Weasku Inn. Built in 1924 near the banks of the Rogue River, the inn welcomes guests with 5 Lodge Rooms, 11 River Front Cabins, 1 A-Frame Cabin and a 3-bedroom River House.

The Weasku Inn
5560 Rogue River Hwy
Grants Pass, OR 97527
541-471-8000

Before You Leave:

Fill your gas tank in Gold Beach or Brookings, if you're heading south.

PHONE NUMBERS - OREGON ROAD TRIPS - OREGON COAST EDITION

- Bandon Dunes Golf Resort: 1-866-311-3636
- Cannery Pier Hotel & Spa: 503-325-4996
- Cannon Beach Hotel: 503-436-1392
- Carrie's Whale Watching EcoExcursions: 541-912-6734
- Channel House: 541-765-2140
- Coos Bay Manor B & B: 541-290-9779 or 541-269-1224
- Depoe Bay Whale Watching Center: 541-765-3304
- Drift Inn Hotel & Café: 541-547-4477
- Heceta Head Lighthouse B & B: 541-547-3696 or 1-866-547-3696
- Jerry's Rogue River Jet Boat Tours: 800-451-3645
- Les Schwab Tire Center – Astoria/Warrenton: 503-861-3252
- Les Schwab Tire Center – Seaside: 503-738-9243
- Les Schwab Tire Center – Tillamook: 503-842-5543
- Les Schwab Tire Center – Newport: 541-265-6604
- Les Schwab Tire Center – Florence: 541-997-7178
- Les Schwab Tire Center – Coos Bay: 541-267-3163
- Marine Discovery Cruise: 541-265-6200
- Ocean House Bed & Breakfast: 541-265-3888
- Old Wheeler Hotel: 503-368-6000
- Oregon Coast Aquarium: 541-867-3474
- Oregon Coast Railriders: 541-786-6165
- Oregon Coast Scenic Railroad: 503-842-7972
- Pacific Reef Resort: 541-247-6658
- Rogue River Lodge at Snag Patch: 541-247-0101
- Sheltered Nook Tiny Homes: 503-805-5526
- Stephanie Inn: 503-436-2221 or 855-977-2444
- Sylvia Beach Hotel B & B: 541-265-5428
- Tu Tu' Tun Lodge: 541-247-6664
- Weasku Inn: 541-471-8000
- Whale Cove Inn: 541-765-4300
- Wolf Creek Inn: Via Reserve America – 800-452-5687

WHALE WATCHING ON THE OREGON COAST

Our thanks to Tiffany Boothe of Oregon State Parks & Recreation, as well as VisitTheOregonCoast.com for this article.

Whale watching is a year-round activity on the Oregon Coast with gray whales by far the most commonly seen. Whale watching is not difficult, but a few tips make it easier. Any location with an ocean view may yield whale sightings, and morning light with the sun at your back is best. First locate whale spouts with your naked eye; then focus more closely with binoculars. For an even closer view, try whale watching from a charter boat. And some people prefer the view from above—from an airplane or helicopter. Both charter boats and air services are available (and listed here). And, of course, calmer days are best, whether by land, sea, or air.

Gray Whale Migration

Gray whales migrate South from their feeding grounds in the Bering and Chukchi seas around Alaska from mid-December through January. They are heading to their breeding grounds in Baja California, Mexico, where warm-water lagoons become nurseries for expectant mothers. Then from late March to June the whales migrate north back to Alaska. On each trip, approximately 18,000 gray whales pass close to the Oregon Coast.

On the trip down, these giant mammals head South on a direct course, move quickly, and mostly stay about 5 miles offshore. At their peak, about 30 whales pass by each hour. Coming back, the whales travel much more leisurely and stay closer to shore—within a half mile is not unusual. The non-breeding males and females lead the way back with some early birds starting in late February. They may even pass stragglers still heading south. The northward migration continues at a slower pace and mothers with young don't usually appear until May.

Resident Gray Whales in Summer

Some gray whales do not continue on to Alaskan waters but stay off the coast of Oregon between June and November. These part-time residents number about 200. About 60 whales are seen repeatedly off the central coast and have been photographed and identified. Of these, about 40 hang out between Lincoln City and Newport each year because that seems to be what the food supply will support.

Whale Watching Spoken Here Program

Each year peak migration times coincide with people's vacation times. The *Whale Watching Spoken Here* program takes advantage of this coincidence with three weeks of assisted whale watching: the first is the week between Christmas and New Year's, the second is during the last week in March, and the third is the last week of August through the first Monday in September. The summer whale watch locations are those along the central coast and focus on the part-time resident whales. During each whale-watch week hundreds of volunteers man 26 sites along the coast from Ilwaco, Washington to Crescent City, California.

Spy Hopping and Breaching Behavior

The two whale behaviors that get people excited are spy hopping—where the head sticks straight up out of the water—and breaching—where 1/2 to 3/4 of the body length comes up out of the water and falls on its side or back causing a tremendous splash.

Where to Spot Whales

From north to south, here are 23 *Whale Watching Spoken Here* sites. With or without a volunteer to assist, these are the best locations along the coast to spot whales.

1. Ecola State Park
2. Neahkahnie Mountain Historic Marker Turnout on Highway 101
3. Cape Meares State Scenic Viewpoint
4. Cape Lookout State Park – 2.5 mile hike to the tip of the Cape
5. Cape Kiwanda at Pacific City
6. Inn at Spanish Head - Lobby on the 10th floor
7. Boiler Bay State Scenic Viewpoint
8. The Whale Watching Center/Depoe Bay Sea Wall
9. Rocky Creek State Scenic Viewpoint
10. Cape Foulweather
11. Devil's Punchbowl State Natural Area
12. Yaquina Head Outstanding Natural Area
13. Don Davis City Park
14. Cape Perpetua Interpretive Center
15. Cook's Chasm Turnout
16. Umpqua Lighthouse, near Umpqua Lighthouse State Park
17. Shore Acres State Park
18. Face Rock Wayside State Scenic Viewpoint
19. Cape Blanco Lighthouse, near Cape Blanco State Park
20. Battle Rock Wayfinding Point, Port Orford
21. Cape Sebastian
22. Cape Ferrelo
23. Harris Beach State Park, Brookings, Oregon

Whale Watching by Sea and Air

Whale watching is better in the spring through fall months when the seas and skies offer smoother conditions. The following is a list of both charterboats and flight services offered along the Oregon Coast...

Charterboats:

- Rockaway Beach - Linda Sue III Charters & Troller, 503-355-3419
- Garibaldi - D&D Charters (spring through fall), 800-900-HOOK (4665)

- Depoe Bay – Whale Research EcoExcursions – 541-912-6743 - www.OregonWhales.com
- Depoe Bay - Tradewinds Charters, 800-445-8730
- Depoe Bay - Dockside Charters, also have Zodiacs, 800-733-8915
- Newport - Marine Discovery Tours (spring through fall), 65-foot Discovery, 800-903-BOAT (2628)
- Newport - Bayfront Charters, 800-828-8777
- Newport - Sea Gull Charters, 800-865-7441
- Newport Tradewinds, 800-676-7819
- Newport Marina Store and Charters, South Beach, 541-867-4470
- Charleston - Betty Kay Charters, 800-752-6303
- Brookings - Tidewind Sportfishing, 800-799-0337

Scenic & Whale-Watch Flights:

Most flights carry from one to three passengers. Rates vary and reservations are recommended but not always required. All flights are dependent upon the weather.

- Twiss Air Service/Astoria Flight Center, one to three passengers, Astoria 503-861-1222
- Tillamook Air Tours, one to four passengers, 503-842-1942
- Florence Aviation, one passenger, Florence 541-997-8069
- Crosswind Air Tours, two or three passengers (minimum two), Florence 541-997-8069
- Coos Aviation, one to three passengers, North Bend 541-756-5181
- Frank's Flight Service, one to three passengers, Bandon 541-347-2022

YOUR NEXT OREGON ROAD TRIP IS READY!

Oregon Road Trips – Northeast Edition

Just as with this road trip guide, we've already laid out an exciting 9-day journey through Northeast Oregon's scenic backroads and byways for you. Along the way, you'll ride aboard a historic steam train, wander Oregon ghost towns, ascend in a cable tram to over 8,000', stay at the 1907 Balch Hotel, board the Sumpter Valley Dredge, explore Cottonwood Canyon, ride the rails on a 2-seater, explore unique shops, eat at great restaurants, meet friendly people and so much more!

Your Northeast Oregon road trip awaits, and it's already planned for you!

Available Now at Retailers Throughout Oregon, Discover-Oregon.com, and Online

AND ANOTHER GREAT
ROAD TRIP AWAITS!

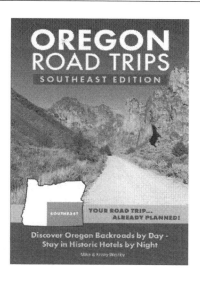

Oregon Road Trips – Southeast Edition

If you enjoyed this Oregon Coast road trip, then you're sure to enjoy exploring remote Southeast Oregon. As with this title, you'll simply turn each page as you motor along and choose which points of interest to stop at and explore during your day's journey, *all while making your way toward that evening's lodging in a historic Oregon hotel.*

You'll drive to the top of 9,734' Steens Mountain, stay in the 1923 Frenchglen Hotel, explore the remote Leslie Gulch, see how stage coaches are built, dig for fossils, hike "Crack in the Ground", look for wild Mustangs, eat at a truly unique and remote Oregon restaurant, marvel at the geologic wonders of the Journey Through Time Scenic Byway and so much more!

Available Now at Retailers Throughout Oregon, Discover-Oregon.com, and Online

EXPLORE
SOUTHWEST OREGON!

Road Trip Oregon's Majestic Mt. Hood!

Oregon Road Trips – Mt. Hood Edition

An alpine Oregon Road Trip adventure is waiting for you!

Set out on an exciting Oregon road trip where every night ends at a charming historic hotel, finishing with majestic Timberline Lodge at 6,000' on the south shoulder of Mt. Hood! Explore the Historic Columbia River Highway, hike the unique Mosier Tunnels route, visit Oregon's oldest bookstore, walk among the Columbia River Gorge's colorful spring wildflowers, fly in a vintage 2-seater biplane, ride to over 7,000' on the Magic Mile Chairlift, discover the rustic and remote 1889 Cloud Cap Inn on Mt. Hood's eastern flank, and so much more.

Available Now at Retailers Throughout Oregon, Discover-Oregon.com, and Online

DISCOVER THE
COLUMBIA RIVER GORGE!

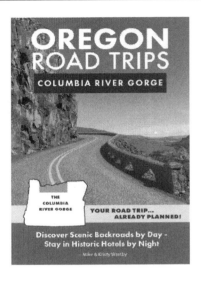

Oregon Road Trips –
Columbia River Gorge Edition

Journey along the Historic Columbia River Highway deep into the Columbia River Gorge, where you'll spend five days seeing the Gorge's majestic waterfalls, flying in a vintage 2-seater biplane, hiking through the historic Mosier Tunnels, stepping into the void on an exciting zip line tour, walking amidst the Gorge's beautiful spring wildflowers, finding your next book at Oregon's oldest bookstore, and even spotting Giraffes, Zebras, Camels, Ostriches and more!

Your Columbia River Gorge road trip awaits, and it's already planned for you!

Available Now at Retailers Throughout Oregon, Discover-Oregon.com, and Online

WHAT TO
SEE, DO & EXPLORE
ON THE OREGON COAST!

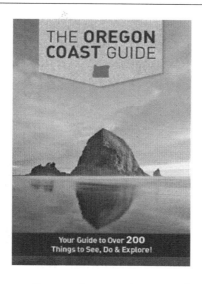

At 363 miles long, Oregon's scenic coastline is filled with countless natural wonders and attractions to see, do, and explore. Hike to a high bluff to watch for whales, walk a long sandy beach, explore a historic lighthouse, catch a live Dungeness crab, join in the fun of a sandcastle building contest, even ride aboard an old-fashioned steam train. The problem is...how do you uncover all of these activities to get the most out of your trip? The solution is the new *Oregon Coast Guide.* Inside these pages, you'll discover over 200 fun and adventurous things to see, do and explore while visiting the Oregon Coast, complete with descriptions, photos, maps, tips, a whale watching guide and much more.

Available Now at Retailers Throughout Oregon, Discover-Oregon.com, and Online

EXPLORE THE
COLUMBIA RIVER GORGE

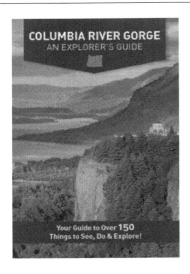

Cutting a deep gorge between Oregon and Washington, the majestic Columbia River Gorge is filled with scenic vistas, graceful waterfalls, amazing attractions, captivating history, and countless adventures, and they are all waiting for you in the *Columbia River Gorge – An Explorer's Guide.* With this guide you'll discover the many waterfalls of "Waterfall Alley", walk among the gorge's colorful spring wildflowers, fly in a vintage 2-seater biplane over Mt. Hood, see over 300 restored antique motorcars and aeroplanes up close, explore the Hood River "Fruit Loop", hike classic gorge trails, visit Oregon's oldest bookstore, discover some great new cycling roads and routes, watch world-class sailboarding, see giraffes, zebras, camels, and bison, stay a night or two or three at one of the gorge's historic hotels, watch a master glass blower create a stunning trout out of glass, eat the biggest ice cream cone in your life, and so much more!

Available Now at Retailers Throughout Oregon, Discover-Oregon.com, and Online

Discover
Central Oregon

Central Oregon is a big place. To the west, high Cascade lakes and snowy peaks offer a world of alpine adventure, while to the east, the high desert beckons travelers to another world, one filled with thrilling experiences and geological wonders. In between is a land of scenic vistas, majestic waterfalls, amazing attractions, and countless outdoor and indoor adventures just waiting to be explored, and they're all here for you in the new *Central Oregon – An Explorer's Guide!* Use this guide to discover over 150 unique attractions, destinations, and experiences where you'll discover nine thundering waterfalls, set out on a moonlight kayaking adventure, walk among WWII era aircraft, hike through Oregon's high desert, ride a summer chairlift up Mt. Bachelor to enjoy some amazing alpine views, drive to the top of Paulina Peak, watch world-class rock climbing up close, paddleboard and kayak on the slow flowing Deschutes River, explore an ancient lava tube, and much more!

Available Now at Retailers Throughout Oregon, Discover-Oregon.com, and Online

Road Trip
Washington's
Olympic Peninsula

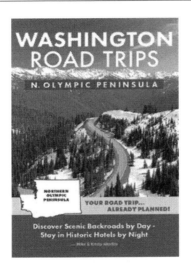

Washington's Olympic Peninsula has always been somewhat of a mystery, but now it's an adventurous and perfectly planned 6-day road trip! Set out to discover this exciting world that varies from high alpine peaks and lofty hiking trails to long sandy beaches and captivating ocean vistas. Stay at and explore the busy Victorian seaport of Port Townsend, visit a historic lighthouse, tour a vintage airplane museum, kayak on the Strait of Juan de Fuca, see majestic Orcas, Humpbacks, and Gray Whales, sleep in your very own castle, stand in the quietest place in the United States, explore unique shops, eat at great restaurants, meet friendly people, and so much more!

Your perfect Northern Olympic Peninsula road trip awaits...and it's already planned for you!

Available Now at Retailers
Throughout Washington and Online

EXPLORE
WASHINGTON'S
OLYMPIC PENINSULA

Now easily discover over 150 things to see, do and explore on Washington's Northern Olympic Peninsula!

The majestic northern Olympic Peninsula is filled with scenic vistas, beautiful beaches, graceful waterfalls, amazing attractions, and countless adventures, and they're all waiting for you in the *Northern Olympic Peninsula – An Explorer's Guide.* Tour a vintage aeroplane museum, visit historic lighthouses, learn how wooden kayaks are made, sleep in your very own castle, see Orcas, Gray Whales, and Humpbacks up close, discover the most beautiful waterfall on the Olympic Peninsula, explore historic Fort Worden, hike stunning Shi Shi and Rialto beaches, hike the captivating Hoh Rainforest, wander old town Port Townsend, and so much more!

Available Now at Retailers
Throughout Washington and Online

Oregon & 1

Oregon, we want to start a grass roots movement.

Imagine if every business in Oregon, large or small, huge or tiny, promoted *at least* one other Oregon business...at no charge, which is completely unrelated to their business.

- A small café promotes a bookstore on its menu.

- A bookstore promotes a historical carousel with a placard by the cash register.

- A historical carousel promotes a tour provider with a small sign near the ticket counter.

- A tour provider promotes a tire store with a mention on its brochures.

- A tire store promotes a local hotel with a note on its invoices.

- A local hotel promotes a theater in the next town over with current showtimes listed at its check-in counter.

- A local theater promotes an auto repair shop with a small sign on its door.

- An auto repair shop promotes a small café with a menu placed in the waiting room.

Creative opportunities to promote Oregon businesses are endless. Better yet, each requires *very little effort or expense* and can start right now...at your business. How do you decide who to promote? Let your employees pick their favorites and rotate their choices on a regular basis.

With all of us extending a hand to our fellow Oregonians beginning today, we can build a powerful interconnected web that reaches all across the state and cross-promotes thousands and thousands of Oregon businesses every day, thus lifting our state's economy, adding to your neighbor's paycheck, and bringing more business to your business.

Oregon and 1!

ABOUT THE AUTHORS

Mike & Kristy Westby on the Oregon Coast

Having been to all six "corners" of Oregon...North, South, East, West, Top and Bottom, (The top of Mt. Hood and the Oregon Coast) we decided it would be fun to take off on a series of multi-day road trips throughout the state. During our journeys, we have been surprised by the number of people we've met who have said they've always wanted to do the same thing, but they've never known where to start. What routes do you take? What places do you see? How do you find them? Where do you stay? *How do you even begin?!* With that in mind, we decided to write our road trip guides so other like-minded souls can easily benefit from the knowledge we've gleaned over the years and set out on their own adventures.

WE RECOMMEND
OREGON SMALL BUSINESSES...

Lifting Oregon Out of the Mud – Building the Oregon Coast Highway

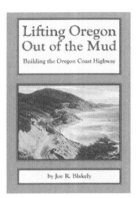

If you'd like to learn more about the engineering and construction of Oregon's impressive coastal bridges, we highly recommend the book *Lifting Oregon Out of the Mud – Building the Oregon Coast Highway*, by Joe R. Blakely. Look for it at gift shops and bookstores along the coast, as well as online. www.Powells.com

75 Classic Rides: Oregon

From an after-work ride through Portland's neighborhood streets or a family cycle along the flat Willamette Valley Scenic Bikeway, to a multi-day tour in the salty breezes of the Oregon coast—if you're seeking the best bike trails in Oregon, you'll find plenty of blacktop bliss in Jim Moore's *75 Classic Rides: Oregon*.

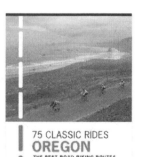

Les Schwab Tire Centers

If you're on the road and have a flat tire, brake issues or a similar problem, we highly recommend the very helpful folks at your nearby Les Schwab Tire Center. There are 10 locations along the Oregon Coast, and you'll find some of their phone numbers listed on Page 189.

Are You a Disneyland Fan?

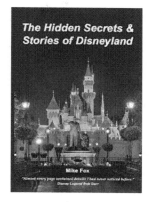

Enjoy a fascinating and entertaining book which reveals over 250 of the hidden secrets and story elements that the Disney Imagineers have purposely hidden for Disneyland guests to find and enjoy, complete with 225 photos!

Available online, as well as at the prestigious Walt Disney Family Museum, the Walt Disney Boyhood Home, and the Walt Disney Hometown Museum.

Want Even More Disneyland Secrets?

Discover the in-depth stories behind 50 magical story elements of Disneyland, *many of which are published here for the very first time.* Compiled from extensive research and lengthy interviews with Disney Legends, Imagineers, and other Disney notables.

Available online and at Disney museums.

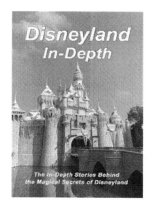

Are You a Walt Disney World Fan?

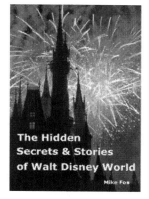

See and experience Walt Disney World in an entirely new way! Written by Oregon author Mike Fox, *The Hidden Secrets & Stories of Walt Disney World* reveals over 500 of the fun and oftentimes whimsical secret story elements that the Disney Imagineers have hidden throughout all four parks. Complete with 400+ photos.

Available online and at Disney museums.

Camp Attitude

"Changing lives one camper at a time!"

Camp Attitude provides a welcoming camp experience for disabled youth and their families. Here, children with special needs can participate in all of the fun, games, excitement and interaction of a thrilling week-long "summer camp" experience, all for a nominal fee, thanks to donations from contributors who enjoy seeing a smile on a child's face...and a squirt gun in their hand!

Camp Attitude is a faith-based non-profit organization, and donations may be made by visiting their web site at www.CampAttitude.org

Camp Attitude
45829 S Santiam Hwy
Foster, OR 97345
541-401-1052

Antiques & Oddities

A popular Columbia River Gorge "antiques destination" for over 20 years, Antiques & Oddities in Bingen, WA is home to an eclectic collection of quality antiques from near and far, including Asia and Europe. Stop in when you're in the Gorge, and be sure to make your way downstairs to check out their latest arrivals.

Antiques & Oddities
211 W. Steuben Street
Bingen, WA 98605

Made in the USA
Middletown, DE
21 February 2022

61390572R00117